SELECTED POEMS

BY

WILLIAM J. GRAYSON

W. J. Grayson

SELECTED POEMS

BY

WILLIAM J. GRAYSON

Selected and Compiled by
MRS. WILLIAM H. ARMSTRONG
(his daughter)

New York and Washington
THE NEALE PUBLISHING COMPANY
1907

CONTENTS

INTRODUCTION

The poems presented in this volume have been selected from a collection of her distinguished father's works by Mrs. William H. Armstrong, of New York and Washington. The author, William J. Grayson, was a Southern gentleman of the old school. He was a representative of that race of men who set high standards of patriotism, Christian manhood, morality and ethics for the guidance of the generation of Americans, particularly at the South, that was born of the men and women who cemented with their blood and tears the enduring foundation upon which has been reared the mighty fabric of this Government. His was a type that now, unhappily for the times and manners, is almost, if not quite, extinct. Mr. Grayson was one of a group of men at Charleston, South Carolina, that with high courage and fortitude strove to avert the pitiful tragedy of the Civil War. Others of this group were James Louis Petigru and Judge King. This trio of names is as familiar and revered in South Carolina as are those of the Hamptons, of Calhoun, of Hayne and of Hamilton. He and Petigru and King pleaded with powerful logic, tempered by loving kindness, against the hazard of war. With prophetic vision they foresaw its results, and from the rigors of these they tried earnestly to protect their people. But when the people and the State they loved plunged the nation into bloody strife they, like Robert E. Lee, cast their fortunes with the South. None of them lived to witness the full effects of the war. Is it too much to believe that to men of their mold death was hastened by the sorrow and affliction of their time and section?

Mr. Grayson was born in Beaufort District, South Carolina, in November, 1788, and died at Newberry on the 4th of October, 1863. His father was an officer in the Continental Army of the Revolution. The son early manifested taste and talent for literature and official life. He was graduated at Columbia College, South Carolina, in 1813; was a commissioner in equity at Beaufort for a long period; subsequently appointed Collector of the Port of Charleston by President Tyler, continued in that office by Polk and Fillmore, and removed for partisan political reasons by President Pierce. He was called to the bar at an early age, and for several years "rode circuit" in the Beaufort District; but the active practice of law proved distasteful to him and he abandoned it to devote his attention to his plantations and public affairs. Before removing to Charleston to accept Federal office he was a member of the State Legislature, and in 1833 represented his district in Congress.

His broad sympathies, no less than his scholarly attainments, are shown in the poem included in this collection, entitled "The Hireling and the Slave." This, like all of his verses, was published for private distribution only, though it sounded so clearly the dominant note of the best thought of the South at the time that it attained wide vogue and wielded an influence which perceptibly softened the asperities of the heated controversy over slavery. "The Hireling and the Slave" was published in 1856, and was dedicated to James Louis Petigru. It aroused discussion in all parts of the country alike for its polemic power and its literary merit. It is included in this collection for two reasons: It displays Mr. Grayson's best style, and its perusal will carry the reader back with startling reality to an era in the life of the country and of the world which no amount of the study of the histories of that time will do. In fervor and stateliness, in pitch and measure it is reminiscent of Alexander Pope's masterful style. Indeed, I make bold to say that no American versifier of this or the elder day has approached in rhythmical sweep or sustained melody the model set by Pope and Dryden as has Mr. Grayson. In "The Hireling and the Slave" there are flights of fancy that reach the highest plane of poetry.

In "Marion" is exhibited the same temperamental quality in the author as in "The Hireling and the Slave." It shows his love of nature as well as his love of the genuine in human character. "Marion" deals with one of the greatest figures of the Revolution. The author runs the gamut of human feeling that impels men to great deeds, and presents a picture that portrays the heroism of the Revolutionary fathers in colors that will endure.

In none of these verses is the real character of Mr. Grayson so finely revealed as in the opening quatrains of this volume. "To My Wife" came from the depths of a heart pure and filled with love for her who was the inspiration of his youth and the benediction of his mellow age. It was not written with the view of publication even for private circulation, but only as a love letter to her to whom it was dedicated. I found it among an unpublished collection of short verses transcribed by Mr. Grayson during the stirring days of '61 or '62 on the yellowing leaves of a quaint old military diary labelled, "Orderly Book. Daniel Stevens, Lieut. Col. Commandant, Regiment of Artillery. 1801." It is instinct with the gentleness and chivalry of the man, and as a specimen of purely sentimental lyric is entitled to high rank.

In "A Sunday Morning's Dream" is found another exhibition of Mr. Grayson's rare power of imagery and felicity of rhyming. So telling an appeal did it make to the devout religious feeling of the time when published in prose as a tract by the Protestant Episcopal Society in 1857 that, at the request of the church authorities, it was converted into verse by Mr. Grayson, and in that form attained a wide circulation. It is included in this collection only because it exhibits his literary versatility as well as the broad sweep of his sentiments.

His other verses in this volume were not selected

because of any pronounced superiority over those not included in the present publication, but chiefly because of the varied character of his talent and attainment which they attest. That he was unconscious of his gifts is evidenced by the indisposition he manifested against his verses being given publicity. He gave himself up to the muse only in idle moments, and apparently had no thought that the children of his fancy would please any but the charmed circle of friends of which he was so attractive and cherished a figure in the days of the Old South.

I believe, as does the publisher, that this little volume will find a host of appreciative readers in all parts of the country, and especially among the sons and daughters of the men and women among whom Mr. Grayson and his compeers strove and wrought masterfully, tenderly, and chivalrously in the darkest days of the nation's history.

J. J. Dickinson.

Washington, D. C.,
August 31, 1907.

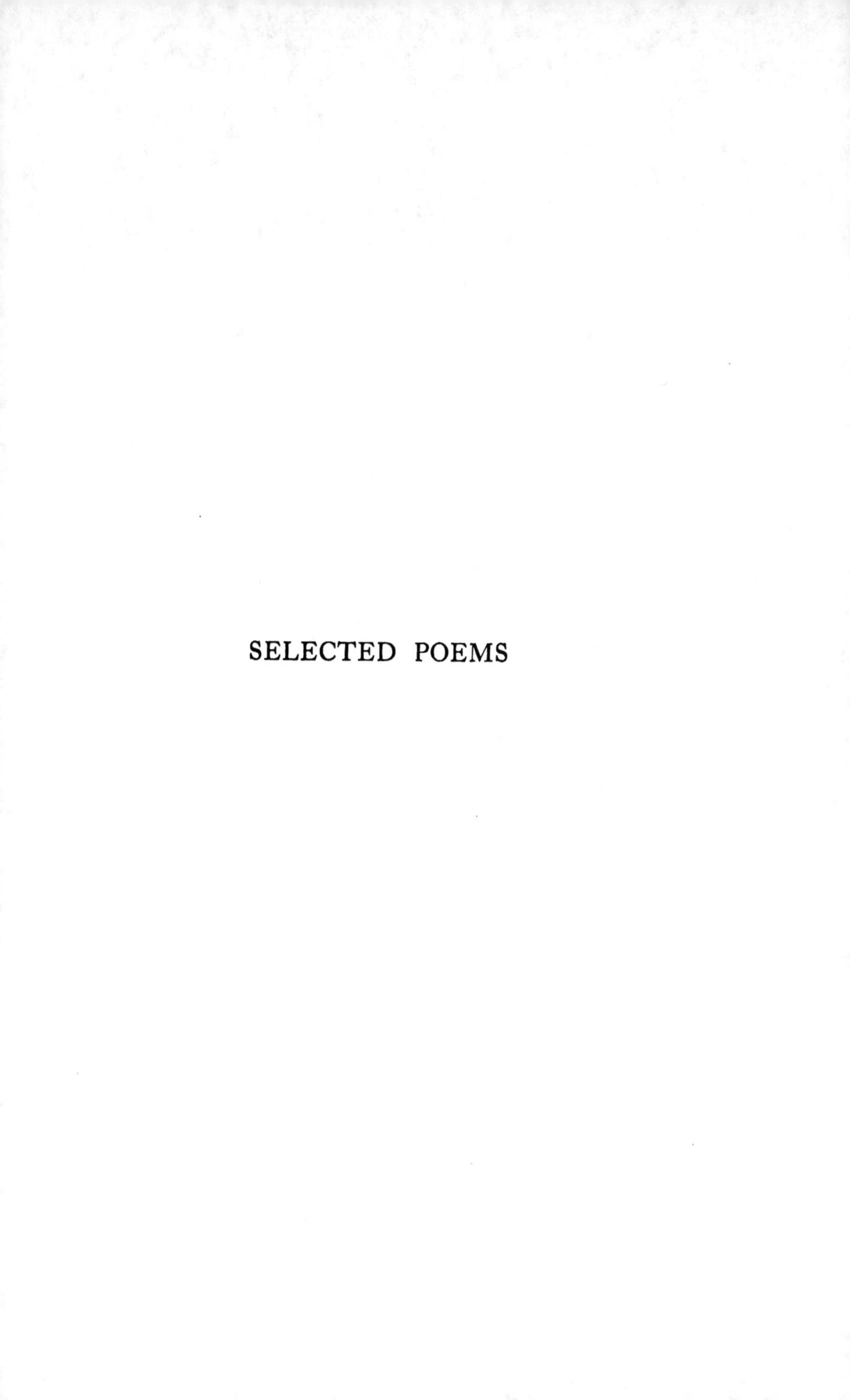

SELECTED POEMS

TO MY WIFE

Dear wife! to Time's unmeasured store
Of countless ages past before
Full forty years are gone and more
Since first we met;
Since, hand in hand, with joy and pride,
We trod life's beaten paths and tried
Its mazy walks as side by side
We tread them yet.

Together we have borne its cares,
Together felt its hopes and fears,
Together wept with mingled tears
Our children dead.
Of infants, sons in youthful bloom
And manhood, hurried to the tomb,
We mourned, ah! how we mourned the doom,
The promise fled.

Not comfortless—the hand that gave,
That took them to an early grave,
That smites, in sorrow, but to save—
The hand of God.
The spirit healed by sorrow broke;
Peace to the troubled waves He spoke,
And bowed our hearts to meet the stroke
And kiss the rod.

Some yet remain to help us bear
Life's burden heavier year by year,
To stay our steps, our path to cheer,
        Our love to claim.
And by their side a little band,
Our children's children, round thee stand,
With tiny fingers clasp thy hand,
        And lisp thy name.

Not all were thorns that met our view;
Life had its summer blossoms too,
And now its autumn bounties strew
        Our downward way.
Content is ours, the modest share
In fortune's gifts of Agur's prayer,
And Faith that nerves the breast to bear
        Life's darkening day.

The lightest touch and stealthiest pace
Of Time have marked thy gentle face,
Have softer made its sweetest grace—
        Its tender smile;
Erect thy form and ready still
Thy dextrous hand and active will
Each household duty to fulfill,
        Each ill beguile.

Still in thy housewife world I trace
Order's first law—a fitting space
For each thing, each thing in its place
Confess thy care.
I see thee at the board preside,
Still ready and with matron pride
Alert and skilful to provide
Its choicest fare.

No cup so fragrant, strong and sweet;
No cloth more white, no tray more neat
Thy household elsewhere ever meet
Where'er they go.
And when the cheering feast is o'er,
Towel and steaming bowl restore
Your cup's bright polish, as before—
No stain they show.

Unwearied yet thy needles shine,
No seam, or stitch, so close as thine;
To mark, trim, cut, in faultless line
No hand so true.
Thy children's children know its aid
In many a dainty garb displayed,
For little rosy strangers made,
And mothers too.

And deeper lines of Time may write
On form and face—if thin and white
The tresses once so darkly bright
About thy brow;
The cheery laugh, the spirit's play
That fairer made the summer day—
If these be hushed, nor light, nor gay
Thy footsteps now.

Yet all unchanged the spirit's form,
The steadfast heart so true and warm,
So prompt to give, in calm or storm,
Its ready aid;
A smile to joy, a tear to woe
Thy varied sympathies bestow
Like bounteous springs that ever flow
In sun or shade.

Assiduous at the sufferer's bed
By day, by night, with noiseless tread,
For fevered lips and aching head,
Thy hands supply
Cool draught or lotion and prepare
Powder, or pill, or coaxing fare,
At fitting times, with watchful care
And sleepless eye.

More blest to give than to receive,
Thy generous heart delights to leave
No wish unmet—you only grieve
        To give no more;
And friendship's token, great or small,
Ring, portrait, curl, or brooch, or shawl,
With careful hand you hoard them all—
        A priceless store.

No gloomy passion ever stirred
Thy gentle breast, no heartless word
That wounds, has child or husband heard
        From year to year.
Love ever comes of love; so soft and mild
Thy winning face, the stranger child
That meets thee seeks thy arms, beguiled
        Of doubt or fear.

Firm too as gentle, when the gale
And gloom of adverse years prevail,
When bent the mast and rent the sail,
        With ready arms;
Not boastingly, nor rough, nor rude,
Of quiet but unflinching mood,
You fight the battle unsubdued,
        In life's alarms.

Bright be its evening, like the flow
Of summer brooks, the mellow glow
Of sunsets, with no sight of woe,
No sound of strife;
And blest, for thee, its close and late;
Truth, hope and love beside thee wait,
And faith disarm the shafts of fate,
Dear faithful wife!

THE HIRELING AND THE SLAVE

PART I

THE ARGUMENT

The state of the hireling and the slave the same substantially—the condition hard labor, the reward subsistence; the hireling does not always obtain the reward—his miseries, starvation, vices, brutality, subjection to militiary service, expulsion from his country; the transportation of the negro from Africa to America a blessing to him—instructs him in mechanic arts, in agriculture; the various products of his industry numerous and useful to the whole world; his improvement not possible in his own country, therefore brought by Providence to this; Abolitionists denouncers of Providence; their object selfish; the negro improved by the master's care only, the Abolitionists do nothing for him; the superiority of the slave over the rest of his race; his security from want; his education not more defective than that of hirelings in Europe; his punishments less severe for similar offenses; master's police more efficient in preserving order and preventing vice.

Part First

Oh, mortal man, that livest here by toil,
  Do not complain of this thy hard estate;
That, like an emmet, thou must ever moil,
  Is a sad sentence of an ancient date;
And, certes, there is for it reason great.

*   *   *   *   *

Withouten that would come a heavier bale,
Loose life, unruly passions, and diseases pale.

Castle of Indolence.

Fallen from primeval innocence and ease,
When thornless fields employed him but to please,*
The laborer toils; and from his dripping brow
Moistens the length'ning furrows of the plow;
In vain he scorns or spurns his altered state,
Tries each poor shift, and strives to cheat his fate;
In vain new-shapes his name to shun the ill—
Slave, hireling, help—the curse pursues him still;
Changeless the doom remains, the mincing phrase
May mock high Heaven, but not reverse its ways.
How small the choice, from cradle to the grave,
Between the lot of hireling, help, or slave!
To each alike applies the stern decree
That man shall labor; whether bond or free,

---

* "Cursed is the ground for thy sake; * * * thorns and thistles shall it bring forth to thee; * * * in the sweat of thy brow shalt thou eat bread."—*Genesis.*

For all that toil, the recompense we claim—
Food, fire, a home and clothing—is the same.
  The manumitted serfs of Europe find
Unchanged this sad estate of all mankind;
What blessing to the churl has freedom proved,
What want supplied, what task or toil removed?
Hard work and scanty wages still their lot,
In youth o'erlabored, and in age forgot,
The mocking boon of freedom they deplore,
In wants and labors never known before.*
  Free but in name—the slaves of endless toil,
In Britain still they turn the stubborn soil,
Spread on each sea her sails for every mart,
Ply in her cities every useful art;
But vainly may the peasant toil and groan
To speed the plow in furrows not his own;
In vain the art is plied, the sail is spread,
The day's work offered for the daily bread;
With hopeless eye, the pauper hireling sees
The homeward sail swell proudly to the breeze,
Rich fabrics wrought by his unequaled hand,
Borne by each breeze to every distant land;
For him, no boon successful commerce yields,
For him no harvest crowns the joyous fields,
The streams of wealth that foster pomp and pride,
No food nor shelter for his wants provide;
He fails to win, by toil intensely hard,

* Pauperism began with the abolition of serfage.—*Westminster Review.*

The bare subsistence—labor's least reward.
 In squalid hut—a kennel for the poor,
Or noisome cellar, stretched upon the floor,
His clothing rags, of filthy straw his bed,
With offal from the gutter daily fed,
Thrust out from Nature's board, the hireling lies:
No place for him that common board supplies,
No neighbor helps, no charity attends,
No philanthropic sympathy befriends;
None heed the needy wretch's dying groan,
He starves unsuccor'd, perishes unknown.
 These are the miseries, such the wants, the cares,
The bliss that freedom for the serf prepares;
Vain is his skill in each familiar task,
Capricious Fashion shifts her Protean mask,
His ancient craft gives work and bread no more,
And Want and Death sit scowling at his door.
 Close by the hovel, with benignant air,
To lordly halls illustrious crowds repair*—
The Levite tribes of Christian love that show
No care nor pity for a neighbor's woe;
Who meet, each distant evil to deplore,
But not to clothe or feed their country's poor;
They waste no thought on common wants or pains,
On misery hid in filthy courts and lanes,
On alms that ask no witnesses but Heaven,
By pious hands to secret suffering given;
Theirs the bright sunshine of the public eye,

* Exeter Hall, the show-place of English philanthropy.

The pomp and circumstance of charity,
The crowded meeting, the repeated cheer,
The sweet applause of prelate, prince, or peer,
The long report of pious trophies won
Beyond the rising or the setting sun,
The mutual smile, the self-complacent air,
The labored speech and Pharisaic prayer,
Thanksgivings for their purer hearts and hands,
Scorn for the publicans of other lands,
And soft addresses—Sutherland's delight,
That gentle dames at pious parties write—
These are the cheats that vanity prepares,
The charmed deceits of her seductive fairs,
When Exeter expands her portals wide,
And England's saintly coteries decide
The proper nostrum for each evil known
In every land on earth, except their own,
But never heed the sufferings, wants, or sins
At home, where all true charity begins.
  There, unconcerned, the philanthropic eye
Beholds each phase of human misery;
Sees the worn child compelled in mines to slave
Through narrow seams of coal, a living grave,
Driven from the breezy hill, the sunny glade,
By ruthless hearts, the drudge of labor made,
Unknown the boyish sport, the hours of play,
Stripped of the common boon, the light of day,
Harnessed like brutes, like brutes to tug, and strain,
And drag, on hands and knees, the loaded wain:

There crammed in huts, in reeking masses thrown,
All moral sense and decency unknown,
With no restraint but what the felon knows,
With the sole joy that beer or gin bestows,
To gross excess and brutalizing strife,
The drunken hireling dedicates his life:
Starved else, by infamy's sad wages fed,
There women prostitute themselves for bread,
And mothers, rioting with savage glee,
For murder'd infants spend the funeral fee;
Childhood bestows no childish sports or toys,
Age neither reverence nor repose enjoys,
Labor with hunger wages ceaseless strife,
And want and suffering only end with life;
In crowded huts contagious ills prevail,
Dull typhus lurks, and deadlier plagues assail,
Gaunt Famine prowls around his pauper prey,
And daily sweeps his ghastly hosts away;
Unburied corses taint the summer air,
And crime and outrage revel with despair.
Torn from the cottage, conscript peasants go
To distant wars, against an unknown foe,
On fields of carnage, at ambition's call,
Perish—the warrior's tool, the monarch's thrall;
Wasted by plagues, unhonored their remains,
They fill a ditch on Danube's marshy plains;
In the night trench of mingled mire and blood,
Swept by cold winds and rains, a ceaseless flood,
Half fed, half clad, the tentless earth their bed,

Reeking with gore in mutual slaughter shed,
Scourged by disease, at every dreary post,
They fall in myriads on Crimea's coast,
Or whelmed in snows on Beresina's shore,
Sleep the long treacherous sleep that wakes no more;
Worn by the toilsome march, the sleety sky,
Crouching in groups, the sinking squadrons lie;
No longer fly the fierce barbarian bands,
But, rapt in visions of far-distant lands,
In their last wild delirious fancies see
The sunny hills—the haunts of infancy,
Green summer meadows, warm unclouded skies,
Welcomes of homely joy and glad surprise,
Till the stern frost-king stops the crimson stream
Of life, and breaks the dying soldier's dream;
Home, friends recede before his icy sway,
The dream of bliss and dreamer fade away,
With frozen hosts, the snowy waste is spread,
And howling wolves feast on the unburied dead.
  Far from their humble homes and native land,
Forced by a landlord's pitiless command,
In uncongenial climes condemned to roam,
That sheep may batten in the peasant's home,
The pauper exiles, from the hill that yields
One parting look on their abandoned fields,
Behold with tears no manhood can restrain,
Their ancient hamlet level'd with the plain:
Then go in crowded ships new ills to find,
More hideous still than those they left behind;

Grim Chol'ra thins their ranks, ship-fevers sweep
Their livid tithes of victims to the deep;
The sad survivors, on a foreign shore,
The double loss of homes and friends deplore,
And beg a stranger's bounty to supply
The food and shelter that their homes deny.
  Yet homebred misery, such as this, imparts
Nor grief nor care to philanthropic hearts;
The tear of sympathy forever flows,
Though not for Saxon or for Celtic woes;
Vainly the starving white, at every door,
Craves help or pity for the hireling poor;
But that the distant black may softlier fare,
Eat, sleep, and play, exempt from toil and care,
All England's meek philanthropists unite
With frantic eagerness, harangue and write;
By purchased tools diffuse distrust and hate,
Sow factious strife in each dependent state,
Cheat with delusive lies the public mind,
Invent the cruelties they fail to find,
Slander, in pious garb, with prayer and hymn,
And blast a people's fortune for a whim.
  Cursed by these factious arts, that take the guise
Of charity to cheat the good and wise,
The bright Antilles, with each closing year,
See harvests fail, and fortunes disappear;
The cane no more its golden treasure yields;
Unsightly weeds deform the fertile fields;
The negro freeman, thrifty while a slave,

Loosed from restraint becomes a drone or knave;
Each effort to improve his nature foils,
Begs, steals, or sleeps and starves, but never toils;
For savage sloth mistakes the freedom won,
And ends the mere barbarian he begun.
  Then, with a face of self-complacent smiles,
Pleased with the ruin of these hapless isles,
And charmed with this cheap way of gaining heaven
By alms at cost of other countries given—
Like Nathan's host, who hospitably gave
His guest a neighbor's lamb his own to save,
Clarkson's meek school beholds with eager eyes,
In other climes, new fields of glory rise,
And heedless still of home, its care bestows,
In other lands, on other negro woes.
  Hesperian lands, beyond the Atlantic wave,
Home of the poor and refuge of the brave,
Who, vainly striving with oppression fly
To find new homes beneath a happier sky;
Hither, to quiet vale or mountain side,
Where Peace and Nature undisturbed abide,
In humble scenes unwonted lore to learn,
Patriot and prince their banished footsteps turn;
The exiled Bourbon finds a place of rest,
And Kossuth comes, a nation's thankless guest;
Here, driven by bigots to their last retreat,
All forms of faith a safe asylum meet,
Each as it wills, untouched by former fears,
Its prayer repeats, its cherished altar rears:

Scorned by all tongues, assailed by every hand,
Alien and outcast from his promised land,
From Carmel's heights and Sion's holier hill,
By God's decree a ceaseless wanderer still,
The Hebrew finds, his long oppression past,
A grateful home of equal laws at last;
The Jesuit's zeal, in this secure abode,
No hostile edict fears, nor penal code,
And Luther's followers, in their Western home,
Like Bachman, scorn the bulls and fires of Rome.
To exile flying from a perjured state,
From royal bigotry and papal hate,
The Huguenot, among his ancient foes,
Found shelter here and undisturbed repose;
Sad the long look the parting exile gave
To France receding on the rising wave!
Her daisied meads shall smile for him no more,
Her orchards furnish no autumnal store,
With memory's eye alone the wanderer sees
The vine-clad hills, the old familiar trees,
The castled steep, the noonday village shade,
The trim quaint garden where his childhood played;
No more he joins the labor of the fields,
Or shares the joy the merry vintage yields;
Gone are the valley homes, by sparkling streams
That long shall murmur in the exile's dreams,
And temples where his sires were wont to pray,
With stern Farel and chivalrous Mornay—
Scenes with long-treasured memories richly fraught,

Where Sully counseled, where Coligni fought,
And Henri's meteor plume in battle shone,
A beacon-light to victory and a throne.
These are all lost; but, smiling in the West,
Hope, still alluring, calms the anxious breast;
And dimly rising through the landward haze,
New forms of beauty court his wistful gaze:
The level line of strand that brightly shines
Between the rippling waves and dusky pines,
A shelving beach that sandy hillocks bound,
With clumps of palm and fragrant myrtle crowned;
Low shores, with margins broad of marshy green,
Bright winding streams the grassy wastes between,
Wood-crested islands that o'erlook the main,
Like dark hills rising on a verdant plain;
Trees of new beauty, climbing to the skies,
With various verdure meet his wondering eyes:
Gigantic oaks, the monarchs of the wood,
Whose stooping branches sweep the rising flood,
And, robed in solemn draperies of moss,
To stormy winds their proud defiance toss;
Magnolias bright with glossy leaves and flowers,
Fragrant as Eden in its happiest hours;
The gloomy cypress, towering to the skies,
The maple, loveliest in autumnal dyes,
The palm armorial, with its tufted head,
Vines over all in wild luxuriance spread,
And columned pines, a mystic wood, he sees,
That sigh and whisper to the passing breeze:

Here, with determined will and patient toil,
From wood and swamp he wins the fertile soil;
To every hardship stern endurance brings,
And builds a fortune undisturbed by kings;
Fair fields of wealth and ease his children find,
Nor heed the homes their fathers left behind.
  Companions of his toil, the axe to wield,
To guide the plow, and reap the teeming field,
A sable multitude unceasing pour
From Niger's banks and Congo's deadly shore;
No willing travelers they, that widely roam,
Allured by hope to seek a happier home,
But victims to the trader's thirst for gold,
Kidnapped by brothers, and by fathers sold,
The bondsman born, by native masters reared,
The captive band in recent battle spared;
For English merchants bought; across the main,
In British ships, they go for Britain's gain;
Forced on her subjects in dependent lands,
By cruel hearts and avaricious hands,
New tasks they learn, new masters they obey,
And bow submissive to the white man's sway.
  But Providence, by his o'erruling will,
Transmutes to lasting good the transient ill,
Makes crime itself the means of mercy prove,
And avarice minister to works of love.
In this new home, whate'er the negro's fate—
More blessed his life than in his native state!
No mummeries dupe, no Fetich charms affright,

Nor rites obscene diffuse their moral blight;
Idolatries, more hateful than the grave,
With human sacrifice, no more enslave;
No savage rule its hecatomb supplies
Of slaves for slaughter when a master dies:
In sloth and error sunk for countless years
His race has lived, but light at last appears —
Celestial light: religion undefiled
Dawns in the heart of Congo's simple child;
Her glorious truths he hears with glad surprise,
And lifts his eye with rapture to the skies;
The noblest thoughts that erring mortals know,
Waked by her influence, in his bosom glow;
His nature owns the renovating sway,
And all the old barbarian melts away.
  And now, with sturdy hand and cheerful heart,
He learns to master every useful art,
To forge the axe, to mould the rugged share,
The ship's brave keel for angry waves prepare:
The rising wall obeys his plastic will,
And the loom's fabric owns his ready skill.
  Where once the Indian's keen, unerring aim,
With shafts of reed transfixed the forest game,
Where painted warriors late in ambush stood,
And midnight war-whoops shook the trembling wood,
The negro wins, with well directed toil,
Its various treasures from the virgin soil;
Swept by his axe the forests pass away,
The dense swamp opens to the light of day;

The deep morass of reeds and fetid mud,
Now dry, now covered by the rising flood,
In squares arranged by lines of bank and drain,
Smiles with rich harvests of the golden grain,
That, wrought from ooze by nature's curious art
To pearly whiteness, cheers the negro's heart,
Smokes on the master's board in goodly show,
A mimic pyramid of seeming snow,
And borne by commerce to each distant shore,
Supplies the world with one enjoyment more.
  On upland slopes, with jungle lately spread,
The lordly maize uplifts its tasseled head;
Broad, graceful leaves of waving green appear,
And shining threads adorn the swelling ear —
The matchless ear, whose milky stores impart
A feast that mocks the daintiest powers of art
To every taste; whose riper bounty yields
A grateful feast amid a thousand fields,
And sent, on mercy's errand, from the slave
To starving hirelings, saves them from the grave.
  In broader limits, by the loftier maize,
The silk-like cotton all its wealth displays:
Through forked leaves, in endless rows unfold
Gay blossoms tinged with purple dyes and gold;
To suns autumnal bursting pods disclose
Their fleeces, spotless as descending snows;
These, a rich freight, a thousand ships receive,
A thousand looms with fairy fingers weave;
And hireling multitudes in other lands

Are blessed with raiment from the negro's hands.
  Nor these alone they give; their useful toil
Lures the rich cane to its adopted soil—
The luscious cane, whose genial sweets diffuse
More social joys than Hybla's honeyed dews;
Without whose help no civic feast is made,
No bridal cake delights—without whose aid
China's enchanting cup itself appears
To lose its virtue, and no longer cheers,
Arabia's fragrant berry idly wastes
Its pure aroma on untutored tastes,
Limes of delicious scent and golden rind
Their pungent treasures unregarded find,
Ices refresh the languid belle no more,
And their lost comfits infant worlds deplore.
  The weed's soft influence, too, his hands prepare,
That soothes the beggar's grief, the monarch's care,
Cheers the lone scholar at his midnight work,
Subdues alike the Russian and the Turk,
The saint beguiles, the heart of toil revives,
Ennui itself of half its gloom deprives,
In fragrant clouds involves the learned and great,
In golden boxes helps the toils of state,
And, with strange magic and mysterious charm,
Hunger can stay, and bores and duns disarm.
  These precious products in successive years,
Trained by a master's skill, the negro rears;
New life he gives to Europe's busy marts,
To all the world new comforts and new arts;

Loom, spinner, merchant, from his hands derive
Their wealth, and myriads by his labor thrive;
While slothful millions, hopeless of relief,
The slaves of pagan priest and brutal chief,
Harassed by wars upon their native shore,
Still lead the savage life they led before.
  Instructed thus, and in the only school
Barbarians ever know—a master's rule,
The negro learns each civilizing art
That softens and subdues the savage heart,
Assumes the tone of those with whom he lives,
Acquires the habit that refinement gives,
And slowly learns, but surely, while a slave,
The lessons that his country never gave.
  There tropic suns with fires unceasing pour
A baleful radiance on the deadly shore;
Foul vapors guard it; a remorseless host
Of phrensied fevers sentinel the coast,
Brood on the stream, the forest depths invade,
Lurk with alluring slumber in the shade,
Pursue the stranger that attempts to brave
Their fatal power, and hurl him to the grave.
  Science in vain her healing hand applies,
From the dread coast refining Commerce flies,
The savage gloom no foreign lights remove
Of arts or arms that conquer to improve;
Nor yet beneath these unpropitious skies,
Of native growth, can art or science rise;
While states and empires—an august array,

In ruin glorious, flourish and decay;
No sable muses here, with voice divine,
Speak the charmed words that soften and refine,
No black Prometheus with heroic heart
Wins and bestows the shining gifts of art,
Bondsman of Fetich violence and lust,
A slave of slaves, the negro licks the dust,
Unchanged since Heaven's creative word outspread
The seas, and heaved the mountains from their bed.
  Hence is the negro come, by God's command,
For wiser teaching to a foreign land;
If they who brought him were by Mammon driven,
Still have they served, blind instruments of Heaven;
And though the way be rough, the agent stern,
No better mode can human wits discern,
No happier system wealth or virtue find,
To tame and elevate the negro mind:
Thus mortal purposes, whate'er their mood,
Are only means with Heaven for working good;
And wisest they who labor to fulfill,
With zeal and hope, the all-directing will,
And in each change that marks the fleeting year,
Submissive see God's guiding hand appear.
  Such was the lesson that the patriarch taught,
By brothers sold, a slave to Egypt brought,
When, throned in state, vicegerent of the land,
He saw around his guilty brethren stand,
On each pale, quivering lip, remorse confess'd,
And fear and shame in each repentant breast;

No flashing eye rebuked, no scathing word
Of stern reproof the trembling brothers heard;
Love only glistened in the prophet's eyes,
And cheering told the purpose of the skies;
"Grieve not your hearts," he said, "dismiss your fear,
It was not you, but Heaven, that sent me here;
His chosen instrument, I come to save
Pharaoh's proud hosts and people from the grave,
From Egypt's ample granaries to give
Their hoarded stores, and bid the dying live:
To Israel's race deliverance to impart,
And soothe the sorrows of the old man's heart:*
This Heaven's high end; to further the design,
As he commands, your humble task and mine."
So here, though hid the end from mortal view,
Heaven's gracious purpose brings the negro too;
He comes by God's decree, not chance nor fate,
Not force, nor fraud, nor grasping scheme of state,
As Joseph came to Pharaoh's storied land,
Not by a brother's wrath, but Heaven's command;
What though humaner Carlisle disapprove,
Profounder Brougham† his vote of censure move,
And Clarkson's friends with modest ardor show
How much more wisely they could rule below,
Prove, with meek arrogance and lowly pride,
What ills they could remove, what bliss provide,

---

* "That old man, of whom ye spake, is he yet alive?"
† "Pronounced Broom from Trent to Tay."—BYRON.

Forestall the Saviour's mercy, and devise
A scheme to wipe all tears from mortal eyes;
Yet time shall vindicate Heaven's humbler plan,
"And justify the ways of God to man."
But if, though wise and good the purposed end,
Reproach and scorn the instrument attend;
If, when the final blessing is confess'd,
Still the vile slaver all the world detest;
Arraign the states that sent their ships of late
To barter beads and rum for human freight,
That claimed the right, by treaty to provide
Slaves for themselves, and half the world beside,
And from the Hebrew learned the craft so well,
Their sable brothers to enslave and sell.
Shame and remorse o'erwhelmed the Hebrew race,
And penitence was stamped on every face;
But modern slavers, more sagacious grown,
In all the wrong, can see no part their own;
They drag the negro from his native shore,
Make him a slave, and then his fate deplore;
Sell him in distant countries, and, when sold,
Revile the buyers, but retain the gold:
Dext'rous to win, in time, by various ways,
Substantial profit and alluring praise,
By turns they grow rapacious and humane,
And seize alike the honor and the gain:
Had Joseph's brethren known this modern art,
And played with skill the philanthropic part,
How had bold Judah raved in freedom's cause,

How Levi cursed the foul Egyptian laws,
And Issachar, in speech or long report,
Brayed at the masters found in Pharaoh's court,
And taught the king himself the sin to hold
Enslaved the brother they had lately sold,
Proving that sins of traffic never lie
On knaves who sell, but on the dupes that buy.
  Such now the maxims of the purer school*
Of ethic lore, where sons of slavers rule;
No more allowed the negro to enslave,
They damn the master, and for freedom rave,
Strange modes of morals and of faith unfold,
Make newer gospels supersede the old,
Prove that ungodly Paul connived at sin,
And holier rites, like Mormon's priest, begin;
There, chief and teacher, Gerrit Smith appears,
There Tappan mourns, like Niobe, all tears,
Carnage and fire mad Garrison invokes,
And Hale, with better temper, smirks and jokes;
There Giddings, with the negro mania bit,
Mouths, and mistakes his ribaldry for wit,
His fustian speeches into market brings,
And prints and peddles all the paltry things;
The pest and scorn of legislative halls,
No rule restrains him, no disgrace appalls;
Kicked from the House, the creature knows no pain,

* The purer school of New England, which sets aside the Constitution and the Gospel, and substitutes Parker for St. Paul, and Beecher and Garrison for the Evangelists.

But crawls, contented, to his seat again,
Wallows with joy in slander's slough once more,
And plays Thersites happier than before;
Prompt from his seat—when distant riots need
The Senate's aid—he flies with railway speed,
Harangues, brags, bullies, then resumes his chair,
And wears his trophies with a hero's air;
His colleagues scourge him; but he shrewdly shows
A profitable use for whips and blows—
His friends and voters mark the increasing score,
Count every lash, and honor him the more.
  There supple Sumner, with the negro cause,
Plays the sly game for office and applause;
What boots it if the negro sink or swim?
He wins the Senate—'tis enough for him.
What though he blast the fortunes of the state
With fierce dissension and enduring hate?
He makes his speech, his rhetoric displays,
Trims the neat trope, and points the sparkling phrase
With well-turned period, fosters civil strife,
And barters for a phrase a nation's life;
Sworn into office, his nice feelings loathe*
The dog-like faithfulness that keeps an oath;
For rules of right the silly crowd may bawl,
His loftier spirit scorns and spurns them all;

* "Is thy servant a dog that he should do this thing?"—Mr. Sumner's answer, when asked whether he would obey the Constitution as interpreted by the authorities of the country.

He heeds nor court's decree nor Gospel light,
What Sumner thinks is right alone is right;
On this sound maxim sires and sons proceed,
Changed in all else, but still in this agreed;
The sires all slavers, the humaner son
Curses the trade, and mourns the mischief done.
For gold they made the negroes slaves, and he
For fame and office seeks to set them free;
Self still the end in which their creeds unite,
And that which serves the end is always right.
  There Greeley, grieving at a brother's woe,
Spits with impartial spite on friend and foe;
His negro griefs and sympathies produce
No nobler fruits than malice and abuse;
To each fanatical delusion prone,
He damns all creeds and parties but his own,
Brawls, with hot zeal, for every fool and knave,
The foreign felon and the skulking slave;
Even Chaplin, sneaking from his jail, receives
The Tribune's sympathy for punished thieves,
And faction's fiercest rabble always find
A kindred nature in the Tribune's mind;
Ready each furious impulse to obey,
He raves and ravens like a beast of prey,
To bloody outrage stimulates his friends,
And fires the Capitol for party ends.
  There Seward smiles the sweet perennial smile,
Skilled in the tricks of subtlety and guile;
The slyest schemer that the world e'er saw;

Peddler of sentiment and patent law;
Ready for fee or faction to display
His skill in either, if the practice pay,
But void of all that makes the frank and brave,
And smooth, and soft, and crafty like the slave;
Soft as Couthon when, versed in civil strife,
He sent his daily victims to the knife,
Women proscribed with calm and gentle grace,
And murdered mildly with a smiling face:
Parental rule in youth he bravely spurned,
And higher law with boyish wit discerned;
A village teacher then, his style betrays
The pedant practice of those learned days,
When boys, not demagogues, obeyed his nod,
His higher law the tear-compelling rod;
While Georgia's guest, a pleasant life he led,
And Slavery fed him with her savory bread,
As now it helps him, in an ampler way,
With spells and charms that factious hordes obey.
  There Stowe, with prostituted pen, assails
One half her country in malignant tales;
Careless, like Trollope, whether truth she tells,
And anxious only how the libel sells,
To slander's mart she furnishes supplies,
And feeds its morbid appetite for lies
On fictions fashioned with malicious art,
The venal pencil, and malignant heart,
With fact distorted, inference unsound,
Creatures in fancy, not in nature found—

Chaste Quadroon virgins, saints of sable hue,
Martyrs, than zealous Paul more tried and true,
Demoniac masters, sentimental slaves,
Mulatto cavaliers, and Creole knaves—
Monsters each portrait drawn, each story told!
What then? The book may bring its weight in gold;
Enough! upon the crafty rule she leans,
That makes the purpose justify the means,
Concocts the venom, and, with eager gaze,
To Glasgow flies for patron, pence, and praise,
And for a slandered country finds rewards
In smiles or sneers of duchesses and lords.
For profits and applauses poor as these,
To the false tale she adds its falser Keys*
Of gathered slanders—her ignoble aim,
With foes to traffic in her country's shame.
Strange power of nature, from whose efforts flow
Such diverse forms as Nightingale and Stowe!
One glares a torch of discord; one a star
Of blessing shines amid the wrecks of war;
One prone to libel; one to deeds of love;
The vulture-spirit one, and one the dove;

---

* Mrs. Stowe has published what she calls a Key to her tale. It is a compilation of all the slanders and crimes among slaveholders; just as she would write a story denouncing matrimony, and make a Key, from the courts or gossiping chronicles, of all the cruelties, murders, and adulteries of husbands and wives, representing the crimes as the normal condition of the relation.

In various joys their various natures deal,
One leaves her home to wound it, one to heal;
That to expose its sorrows, not deplore;
To help and cheer, this seeks a foreign shore.
  Far from her country, where Marmora flows,
On Mercy's errand England's daughter goes,
To tend the suffering sick with woman's care,
To snatch the bleeding soldier from despair;
Bend o'er his couch, his languid head sustain,
With tender hand assuage the pangs of pain,
Watch o'er the dying moments of the brave,
And smooth, at least, his passage to the grave;
Love's labor this, and—hers no common fame!
With the heart's homage millions bless her name.
  Not such with Stowe, the wish or power to please,
She finds no joys in gentle deeds like these;
A moral scavenger, with greedy eye,
In social ills her coarser labors lie;
On fields where vice eludes the light of day,
She hunts up crimes as beagles hunt their prey;
Gleans every dirty nook—the felon's jail,
And hangman's mem'ry, for detraction's tale;
Snuffs up pollution with a pious air,
Collects a rumor here, a slander there;
With hatred's ardor gathers Newgate spoils,
And trades for gold the garbage of her toils.
  In sink and sewer thus, with searching eye,
Through mud and slime unhappy wretches pry;
In fetid puddles dabble with delight,

Search every filthy gathering of the night;
Fish from its depths, and to the spacious bag
Convey with care the black, polluted rag;
With reeking waifs secure the nightly bed,
And turn their noisome stores to daily bread.
These use the negro, a convenient tool,
That yields substantial gain or party rule,
Gives what without it they could never know,
To Chase distinction, courtly friends to Stowe,
To Parker, themes for miracles of rant,
And Beecher blesses with new gifts of cant.
The master's task has been the black to train,
To form his mind, his passions to restrain;
With anxious care and patience to impart
The knowledge that subdues the savage heart,
To give the Gospel lessons that control
The rudest breast, and renovate the soul—
Who does, or gives as much, of all who raise
Their sland'rous cry for foreign pence or praise;
Of all the knaves who clamor and declaim
For party power or philanthropic fame,
Or use the negro's fancied wrongs and woes
At pretty themes for maudlin verse or prose?
Taught by the master's efforts, by his care
Fed, clothed, protected many a patient year,
From trivial numbers now to millions grown,
With all the white man's useful arts their own,
Industrious, docile, skilled in wood and field,
To guide the plow, the sturdy axe to wield,

The negroes schooled by slavery embrace
The highest portion of the negro race;
And none the savage native will compare,
Of barbarous Guinea, with its offspring here.
If bound to daily labor while he lives,
His is the daily bread that labor gives;
Guarded from want, from beggary secure,
He never feels what hireling crowds endure,
Nor knows, like them, in hopeless want to crave,
For wife and child, the comforts of the slave,
Or the sad thought that, when about to die,
He leaves them to the cold world's charity,
And sees them slowly seek the poor-house door—
The last, vile, hated refuge of the poor.
Still Europe's saints, that mark the motes alone
In other's eyes, yet never see their own,
Grieve that the slave is never taught to write,
And reads no better than the hireling white;
Do their own plowmen no instruction lack,
Have whiter clowns more knowledge than the black?
Has the French peasant, or the German boor,
Of learning's treasure any larger store;
Have Ireland's millions, flying from the rule
Of those who censure, ever known a school?
A thousand years and Europe's wealth impart
No means to mend the hireling's head or heart;
They build no schools to teach the pauper white,
Their toiling millions neither read nor write;
Whence, then, the idle clamor when they rave

Of schools and teachers for the distant slave?
  And why the soft regret, the coarse attack,
If Justice punish the offending black?
Are whites not punished? When Utopian times
Shall drive from earth all miseries and crimes,
And teach the world the art to do without
The cat, the gauntlet, and the brutal knout,
Banish the halter, galley, jails, and chains,
And strip the law of penalties and pains;
Here, too, offense and wrong they may prevent,
And slaves, with hirelings, need no punishment:
Till then, what lash of slavery will compare
With the dread scourge that British soldiers bear?
What gentle rule, in Britain's Isle, prevails,
How rare her use of gibbets, stocks, and jails!
How much humaner than a master's whip,
Her penal colony and convict ship!
Whose code of law can darker pages show,
Where blood for smaller misdemeanors flow?
The trifling theft or trespass, that demands
For slaves light penance from a master's hands,
Where Europe's milder punishments are known,
Incurs the penalty of death alone.
  And yet the master's lighter rule insures
More order than the sternest code secures;
No mobs of factious workmen gather here,
No strikes we dread, no lawless riots fear;
Nuns, from their convent driven, at midnight fly,
Churches, in flames, ask vengeance from the sky,

Seditious schemes in bloody tumults end,
Parsons incite, and senators defend,
But not where slaves their easy labors ply,
Safe from the snare, beneath a master's eye;
In useful tasks engaged, employed their time,
Untempted by the demagogue to crime,
Secure they toil, uncursed their peaceful life,
With labor's hungry broils and wasteful strife.*
No want to goad, no faction to deplore,
The slave escapes the perils of the poor.

---

* The late Preston strike lost to the parties—masters and workmen—over two millions of dollars, and ended where it began.

THE HIRELING AND THE SLAVE

PART II

THE ARGUMENT

The hireling in Europe willing to exchange for the security of the slave his own precarious subsistence; the comforts of the slave; his religious enjoyments; his sports and amusements; extinction of the Indian tribes in the country now inhabited by the negro; certainty that the negro would also disappear if not protected by slavery; this fate speedy in temperate climates—as certain, if slower, in tropical countries, habitable by whites; awaits the blacks in Hayti; folly of exchanging the comfort and security of the slave for a certain evil of problematical good; purnoses of African slavery—the cultivation of tropical countries, the improvement of the negro, the civilization of Africa; duty of the master to govern with vigor, but kindness; to regard his part of the work as also assigned by Providence, and to perform it faithfully.

Part Second

See yonder poor o'erlabored wight,
  So abject, mean, and vile,
Who begs a brother of the earth
  To give him leave to toil,
And see his lordly fellow-worm
  The poor petition spurn,
Unmindful though a weeping wife
  And helpless offspring mourn.—Burns.

Where hireling millions toil, in doubt and fear,
For food and clothing all the weary year,
Content and grateful if their masters give
The boon they beg—to labor and to live;
While dreamers task their idle wits to find
A short-hand method to enrich mankind,
And Fourier's scheme or Owen's plans entice
Expectant thousands with some deep device
For raising wages, for abating toil,
And reaping crops from ill-attended soil:
If, while the anxious multitudes appear,
Now glad with hope, now yielding to despair,
A seraph form, descending from the skies,
In mercy sent, should meet their wond'ring eyes,
And, smiling, offer to each suppliant there
The promised good that fills the laborer's prayer—
Food, clothing, freedom from the wants, the cares,
The pauper hireling ever feels or fears;

And, at their death, these blessings to renew,
That wives and children may enjoy them too,
That, when disease or age their strength impairs,
Subsistence and a home should still be theirs—
What wonder would the gracious boon impart,
What grateful rapture swell the peasant's heart!
How freely would the hungry list'ners give
A life-long labor thus secure to live!
And yet the life, so unassailed by care,
So blessed with moderate work, with ample fare,
With all the good the starving pauper needs,
The happier slave on each plantation leads;
Safe from harassing doubts and annual fears,
He dreads no famine in unfruitful years;
If harvests fail from inauspicious skies,
The master's providence his food supplies;
No paupers perish here for want of bread,
Or lingering live, by foreign bounty fed;
No exiled trains of homeless peasants go,
In distant climes, to tell their tales of woe:
Far other fortune, free from care and strife,
For work, or bread, attends the negro's life,
And Christian slaves may challenge as their own,
The blessings claimed in fabled states alone—
The cabin home, not comfortless, though rude,
Light daily labor, and abundant food;
The sturdy health that temperate habits yield,
The cheerful song that rings in every field,
The long, loud laugh, that freemen seldom share,

Heaven's boon to bosoms unapproached by care,
And boisterous jest and humor unrefined,
That leave, though rough, no painful sting behind;
While, nestling near, to bless their humble lot,
Warm social joys surround the negro's cot,
The evening dance its merriment imparts,
Love, with his rapture, fills their youthful hearts,
And placid age, the task of labor done,
Enjoys the summer shade, the winter sun,
And, as through life no pauper want he knows,
Laments no poor-house penance at its close.
 Safe in Ambition's trumpet call to strife,
No conscript fears harass his quiet life,
While the crushed peasant bleeds—a worthless thing,
The broken toy of emperor or king;
Calm in his peaceful home, the slave prepares
His garden-spot, and plies his rustic cares;
The comb and honey that his bees afford,
The eggs in ample gourd compactly stored,
The pig, the poultry, with a chapman's art,
He sells or barters at the village mart,
Or, at the master's mansion, never fails
An ampler price to find and readier sales.
 There when December's welcome frosts recall
The friends and inmates of the crowded hall,
To each glad nursling of the master's race
He brings his present, with a cheerful face
And offered hand; of warm, unfeigning heart,
In all his master's joys he claims a part,

And, true as clansman to the Highland chief,
Mourns every loss, and grieves in all his grief;
When Christmas now, with its abundant cheer
And thornless pleasure, speeds the parting year,
He shares the common joy—the early morn
Wakes hunter, clamorous hound, and echoing horn,
Quick steps are heard, the merry season named,
The loiterers caught, the wonted forfeit claimed,
In feasts maturing busy hands appear,
And jest and laugh assail the ready ear;
Whose voice, than his, more gayly greets the dawn,
Whose foot so lightly treads the frosty lawn,
Whose heart as merrily, where mirth prevails,
On every side the joyous season hails?
Around the slaughtered ox—a Christmas prize,
The slaves assembling stand with eager eyes,
Rouse, with their dogs, the porker's piercing cry,
Or drag its squealing tenant from the sty;
With smile and bow receive their winter dues,
The strong, warm clothing, and substantial shoes,
Blankets adorned with stripes of border red,
And caps of wool that warm the woollier head;
Then clear the barn, the ample area fill,
In the gay jig display their vigorous skill;
No dainty steps, no mincing measures here—
Ellsler's trained graces—seem to float in air,
But hearts of joy and nerves of living steel,
On floors that spring beneath the bounding reel;
Proud on his chair, with magisterial glance

And stamping foot, the fiddler rules the dance;
Draws, if he nods, the still unwearied bow,
And gives a joy no bearded bands bestow;
The triple holiday, on angel wings,
With every fleeting hour a pleasure brings;
No ennui clouds, no coming cares annoy,
Nor wants nor sorrows check the negro's joy.
His, too, the Christian privilege to share
The weekly festival of praise and prayer;
For him the Sabbath shines with holier light,
The air grows balmier, and the sky more bright;
Winter's brief suns with warmer radiance glow,
With softer breath the gales of autumn glow,
Spring with new flowers more richly strews the ground,
And summer spreads a fresher verdure round;
The early shower is past; the joyous breeze
Shakes patt'ring rain-drops from the rustling trees,
And with the sun, the fragrant offerings rise
From Nature's censers to the bounteous skies;
With cheerful aspect, in his best array,
To the far forest church he takes his way;
With kind salute the passing neighbor meets,
With awkward grace the morning traveler greets,
And joined by crowds, that gather as he goes,
Seeks the calm joy the Sabbath morn bestows.
There no proud temples to devotion rise,
With marble domes that emulate the skies,
But bosomed deep in ancient trees, that spread
Their limbs o'er mouldering mansions of the dead,

Moss-cinctured oaks and solemn pines between,
Of modest wood, the house of God is seen,
By shaded springs, that from the sloping land
Bubble and sparkle through the silver sand,
Where high o'er arching laurel blossoms blow,
Where fragrant bays breathe kindred sweets below,
And elm and ash their blended arms entwine
With the bright foliage of the mantling vine:
In quiet chat, before the hour of prayer,
Masters and slaves in scattered groups appear;
Loosed from the carriage, in the shades around,
Impatient horses neigh and paw the ground;
No city discords break the silence here,
No sounds unmeet offend the listener's ear;
But rural melodies of flocks and birds,
The lowing, far and faint, of distant herds,
The mocking-bird, with minstrel pride elate,
The partridge whistling for its absent mate,
The thrush's solitary notes prolong,
Bold, merry blackbirds swell the general song;
The crested cardinal, of scarlet hue,
The jay, with restless wing of softer blue,
The cawing crow—upon the loftiest pine
Cautious and safe—their various voices join.
  When now the pastor lifts his earnest eyes,
And hands outstretched, a suppliant to the skies,
No rites of pomp or pride beguile the soul,
No organs peal, no clouds of incense roll,
But, line by line, untutored voices raise,

Like the wild birds, their simple notes of praise,
And hearts of love, with true devotion, bring
Incense more pure to Heaven's eternal King;
On glorious themes their humble thoughts employ,
And rise transported with no earthly joy;
The blessing said, the service o'er, again
Their swelling voices raise the sacred strain;
Lingering, they love to sing of Jordan's shore,
Where sorrows cease, and toil is known no more.
  Not toil alone the fortune of the slave—
He shares the sports and spoils of wood and wave;
Through the dense swamp, where wilder forests rise
In tangled masses, and shut out the skies,
Where the dark covert shuns the noontide blaze,
With agile step he threads the pathless maze;
The hollow gum with searching eye explores,
Traces the bee to its delicious stores,
The ringing axe with ceaseless vigor plies,
And from the hollow scoops the luscious prize.
  When Autumn's parting days grow cold and brief,
Light hoar-frost sparkles on the fallen leaf,
The breezeless pines, at rest, no longer sigh,
Bright, pearl-like clouds hang shining in the sky,
And on strong pinions, in the clear blue light,
Exulting falcons wheel their towering flight,
With short, shrill cry arrest the cheerful flow
Of song, and hush the frightened fields below.
When to the homestead flocks and herds incline,

Sonorous conchs recall the rambling swine,
And from the fleecy field the setting sun
Sends home the slave, his easy harvest done;
In field and wood he hunts the frequent hare,
The wild hog chases to the forest lair;
Entraps the gobbler; with persuasive smoke
Beguiles the 'possum from the hollow oak;
On the tall pine-tree's topmost bough espies
The crafty coon—a more important prize—
Detects the dodger's peering eyes, that glow
With fire reflected from the blaze below;
Hews down the branchless trunk with practiced hand,
And drives the climber from his nodding stand:
Downward at last he springs, with crashing sound,
Where Jet and Pincher seize him on the ground;
Yields to the hunter the contested spoil,
And pays, with feast and fur, the evening toil.
If breezes sleep, and clouds obscure the light,
The boatman tries the fortune of the night,
Launches the swift canoe—on either side
Dips his light paddle in the sparkling tide;
By bank and marshy isle, with measured force
And noiseless stroke, directs his quiet course;
Still, at the bow, a watchful partner stands,
The leaded meshes ready in his hands,
Prepared and prompt to cast—the torch's beam
Gleams like a gliding meteor on the stream;
Along the shore the flick'ring firelight steals,
Shines through the deep, and all its wealth reveals;

The spotted trout its mottled side displays,
Swift shoals of mullet flash beneath the blaze;
He marks their rippling course; through cold and wet,
Lashes the flashing wave with dextrous net,*
With poised harpoon the bass or drum assails,
And strikes the barb through silv'ry tinted scales.
  On sandy islets, when, in early June,
With lustrous glory looks the full-orbed moon,
And, spreading from the eye, her pearly light
Shines on the billows tremulously bright,
When swelling tides—the winds and waves at rest—
Tempt the shy turtle to her simple nest,
That, scooped in sand, and hid with curious art,
Waits the quick life that summer suns impart,
The negro's watchful step the beach explores,
In the loose sand detects its secret stores,
Pursues the fugitive's slow, cumbrous flight,
And wins his crowning trophy for the night.
  No need has he the poacher's doom to fear,
Himself ensnared, while sedulous to snare;
To him no keeper closes field or wood,
Nor law forbids the riches of the flood;
Shrimp, oyster, mullet, an Apician feast,
Fit for the taste of pampered prince or priest,
He freely takes, nor dreads the partial law
That seeks the boon of Nature to withdraw
From common use, for Fortune's sated son,

---

* "Latum funda jam verberat amnem."

A pastime only for his rod or gun,
Kept for an idler's sport, preserved and fed,
While hungry thousands cry aloud for bread.
  Still braver sports are his when April showers
Give life and beauty to the joyous flowers,
When jasmines, through the wood, to early spring,
In golden cups, their dewy incense bring,
White dogwood blossoms sparkle through the trees,
The grape's wild fragrance scents the morning breeze,
And with the warmer sun and balmier air,
The finny myriads to their haunts repair:
Such sports are his—with ready jest and glee,
Where bold Port Royal spreads its mimic sea;
Far in the north—the length'ning bay and sky
Blent into one—its shining waters lie,
And southward, breaking on the shelving shore,
Meet the sea-wave, and swell its endless roar;
On either hand gay groups of islands show
Their charms reflected in the stream below:
No sunnier lands, no lovelier isles than these,
No happier homes the weary traveler sees!
Hilton's long shore on Ocean's breast reclines,
And rears her headland of majestic pines;
Fenced from the billows by her subject isles,
Touched by the rising sun, St. Helen smiles,
Gleaming afar across the purple bay,
Her sand-hills glitter with the morning ray;
Worn by the tides, reluctant Parris yields
To waves and shallows her receding fields;

Dawes centred lies in marshes broad and green,
Beaufort's dark woods adorn the varying scene,
And Lemon's oak, in lonely grandeur, rears
His form—a giant of a thousand years—
The sole survivor of a Titan race,
A living monument, he marks the place
Where dauntless hearts, Ribault's ill-fated band,
Claimed, as their own, the wide imperial land;
Sent by Coligni's wisdom to explore,
For peaceful homes, this new-discovered shore.
They mark each quiet nook, each grassy glade,
And spreading oak, of broad, inviting shade,
In endless woods, with eager pleasure roam,
And hail with joy the promised Western home;
While chiefs and kings the wondrous stranger greet,
And lay their presents at the white man's feet;
But vain the hope! To this sequestered place
Their ancient foes, the fierce Iberian race,
Through miry swamps and pathless thickets steal,
Murder the heretic with frantic zeal,
Pollute, with Christian blood, the virgin sod,
And prove, by massacre, their love of God.
With better fortune, near the bloodstained grave,
Advent'rous Britons, braving wind and wave,
Guided by Sayle, in merry Charles's reign,
Sought wealth and empire on these shores again;
Weary of storm and calm, of seas and skies,
They watched the rising coast with rapturous eyes,
Trod with delight the fragrance-breathing strand,

And drew new life and vigor from the land,
But, warned by spectral visions of the dead,
From the broad bay and peerless islands fled,
To safer fields their feeble fortunes bore,
And built their state on Ashley's sheltered shore.
Far in the west, where sunset's parting beam
With brighter splendor tints the glassy stream,
Pinckney's green island-home yet bears the name*
Of one whose virtues share his country's fame,
A soldier proved, without reproach or fear,
A statesman skilled new commonwealths to rear,
To field and forum equally inured,
What arms had won, his eloquence secured;
With stern resolve his country to defend,
He spurned the arrogance of foe and friend;
War crowned him with the laurels of the brave,
And civic garlands Peace as amply gave;
With care he watched the anarchy that waits,
In ambushed strength, to crush revolting states,
And strove with zeal, all jealous fears above,
To bind them fast by ties of social love:
In this alone his generous spirit saw
For peace, security, and rule for law,
Safety from border strife, from foreign foe,
And the long ills that feeble nations know.
Here, every work of patriot duty wrought,
His peaceful shades the veteran statesman sought;

---

* The country-seat of Gen. C. C. Pinckney.

With ready anecdote the livelong day,
Or playful wit, he charmed the grave and gay,
And taught the art to brighten and refine,
With cheerful wisdom, life's unmarked decline.
  With ready sympathy he loved to view
The April sports, and to partake them too;
To watch—at early dawn, when skies are bright,
And dews lie sparkling in the early light
On leaf and flower—the sail and glistening oar,
Launched on the bay from every creek and shore,
The favorite rock, the noted shoal to reach,
Their landmarks tracing on the distant beach,
Far as the eye commands the scene around,
Gay fleets glide swiftly on the shining Sound;
With shouts and taunts the daily race is run,
The sail is furled, the wonted station won,
The line prepared, the hook with caution tried,
The various bait with artful care applied:
All eager—slaves and masters—to behold
Their annual prize, with glittering scales of gold,
To feel the line through glowing fingers glide,
Watch where the victim shows his burnished side,
With patient skill his various efforts foil,
And seize, in triumph, on the conquered soil;
Then boast and jest exultingly proclaim
New trophies added to the victor's fame,
And the broad grin and shining face declare
How true a joy the negro sportsmen share.
  Now, with declining day, on every hand,

The loaded boats turn slowly to the land,
Spread the light sail, or ply the bending oar,
And seek warm shelter on the wooded shore:
The boat song's chorus, with its wonted charm,
Imparts new vigor to each sturdy arm;
The camp, the hamlet catch the well-known note,*
Expect the spoil, and hail the welcome boat.
With sharpened appetite, the joyous crews
Prolong their feast of savory steaks and stews,
And join, where camp-fires glimmer through the trees,
The light laugh floating on the western breeze;
Describe the fish and fortunes of the day,
How sly the bite, how beautiful the play;
Tell with the grave face the superstitious charm
That wrought the fisherman success or harm;
Recount the feats of fishing or of fun,
In other days, by older sportsmen done;
In dreams renew their triumphs through the night,
And wake to others with the dawning light.
Not Marshfield's master, in the palmiest day,
For feast or fish could readier skill display,
Chowder expound with more consummate art,
At the full trencher play a manlier part,
Or, more secure from each intrusive care,
The joy participate and feast prepare.
Not Elliott, early trained, with easy skill,
Old Walton's various offices to fill,

* The fishermen from a distance encamp near the plantations among the trees.

The sport to lead, the willing ear beguile,
And charm with rare felicity of style,
The straining line with nicer art employs,
With keener zest the manly sport enjoys,
Or takes the fish and fortunes of the day,
Sunshine or shower, more buoyantly gay.
But if the wayward fish refuse the bait,
If floating lines for slacker tides await,
Its trick and fun the idle moment brings,
From boat to boat light-hearted laughter rings;
The novice starts alarmed, his slumber broke
By the sly veteran's oft-repeated joke,
Or Dupe or Jester, stretched in dreamless sleep,
Lie rocked by billows rolling from the deep,
Fanned by the southern breeze, that on its wings,
From the blue sea refreshing coolness brings:
Now roused by hunger, every hand explores
The well-filled box, and culls its ample stores—
Fish from the morning feast; the bounteous maize,
Of grist or flour, an ampler dish displays;
With appetite unsated to the last,
They feast, and kings may covet the repast.
Or more alert the crew, on pleasure bent,
In the gay race the idle hour is spent;
The anchors lifted from their oozy bed,
The long lines coiled, the snowy canvas spread;
With pennants streaming, on the sparkling bay
Their speed or skill the swifter boats display;
The Gull and Falcon stretch their pointed wings,

Through the light foam the rapid Dolphin springs,
The peerless Nautilus, with broader sail,
Skims the green wave, and courts the fresh'ning gale.
  But other scenes attract the sportsman's gaze,
And turn his wandering thoughts to other days,
When on these streams the Indian's swift canoe,
Light as the gull, to sport or battle flew;
Light as the noisy flocks that meet the eye,
On restless pinions flitting gayly by;
A tameless ocean-brood that love to rove
The shore and sea, but shun the quiet grove,
In idle sport they chase and are pursued,
With sudden dart surprise their minnow food,
The rising diver watch, the well-earned prize
Snatch from his bill with sharp, exulting cries,
Or in the stream their glossy plumage lave,
And sit with graceful lightness on the wave.
  Aloft the fish-hawk wings his wary way,
Stops, turns, and watches the incautious prey;
Quick, as the fish attracts his piercing eye,
With fluttered wings a moment poised on high,
Headlong he plunges with unerring aim,
In iron claws secures the struggling game,
Upward again his joyous flight resumes,
And shakes the water from his ruffled plumes.
  Vain is his joy! The eagle's watch explores
The busy scene from Edings' distant shores;
Perched on the pine or live-oak's blasted height,
His wing half folded, and prepared for flight,

With neck outstretched he sits, and flashing eye
Bent on the hawk that hovers lightly by,
Sees the bold plunge, the shining victim sees,
And spreads his dusky pinions to the breeze;
Swift as the shaft just darted from the bow,
Or the sharp flash that cleaves the clouds below,
The hawk perceives the dread aerial king,
Quails at the shadow of the broad dark wing,
Ceases in circling sweeps to scale the sky,
And drops his treasure with indignant cry;*
Swooping with matchless power and rushing sound,
Before the falling prize can reach the ground,
In graceful curve, the eagle meets his spoil,
The plundered product of another's toil,
Regains his perch that far o'erlooks the main,
Feasts with fierce eye, and holds his watch again.
So the mailed baron, with the dawning light,
Watched the broad valley from his castled height;
If far below, dense clouds of mist between,
The passing burgher's flocks and herds were seen,
The merchant troop from Orient climes returned,
With pearls and gold by toil and peril earned,
Down swooped the pennon from the feudal hold,
And clutched the flocks, the costly gems and gold;
Safe on the rocky perch, in wassail rude
Spent the long night, and watch at morn renewed.
Bright streams and isles, how memory loves to trace

---

* So Audubon interprets the cry to mean.

Its boyish sports in each familiar place,
By wood and wave with joy renewed to dwell,
And live again the life once loved so well:
Still, with the scene, old faces reappear,
Voices, long silent, meet the musing ear,
And many a hamlet, gleaming on the shore,
Recalls a friend whose sports and toils are o'er.
Can ceaseless cares for power and place impart
Scenes such as these to charm and mend the heart?
The blue arch resting on the distant trees,
The bright wave curling to the ocean breeze,
The dewy woods that greet the rising sun,
The clouds that close the golden circuit run,
Rolled in bright masses of a thousand dyes,
A pomp and glory in the western skies.
Here every flower that gems the forest sod
May guide the heart from Nature to its God,
And higher hopes and purer joys bestow
Than the poor slaves of faction ever know,
When demagogues have won, with brazen throat,
The loudest cheer and most triumphant vote.
Even when nor party nor a people's voice,
But Providence itself hath made the choice,
And lifts the man, whom worth and wisdom grace,
To sit in Liberty's supremest place;
Though loved and honored in a nation's eyes,
Though faction's self confess him just and wise,
Still the calm home, where peace and virtue dwell,
Charms with a silent, but a mightier spell;

And Fillmore left, without a sigh, the toys
Of state for homelier but serener joys;
Faithful, like Washington, to order's cause,
And prompt, like him, to vindicate her laws,
Like him, he looked with still reverted eye
To happier scenes than office can supply,
Turned from the noisy hall, the coarse debate,
The curse of patronage and frauds of state,
The caucus juggler and his pliant tool,
The slaves of party and its tyrant rule,
The knavish arts that demagogues employ,
Lies that supplant, and whispers that destroy;
Whose work would shame the honest hand of toil,
Whose love of country means the love of spoil,
Who, for their party, wrong their nearest friends,
Betray that party for their private ends,
Pursue with subtle craft, by fraud and force,
The patriot-trade—the scoundrel's last resource;
Deplore the people's wrong, inflame their rage,
In factious brawls for fancied ills engage,
Hot with unmeasured zeal—till office fills
Their itching palms, and cures all wrongs and ills;
From these he turned—from falsehood, craft, and strife,
To the pure joys that wait on private life
In scenes like this, where forest, stream and sky
Speak in charmed accents to the gazer's eye,
And Nature's voiceless eloquence imparts
Her hopes and joys to renovated hearts.

And even here, if Sorrow finds her way,
If, as they will, these hopes and joys decay,
Nor talents guard, nor charms of temper save,
Nor virtues shield the loved one from the grave;
While worldly turmoil wrings the mourner's heart,
Home's quiet scenes a soothing balm impart,
Faith here has room to spread her heavenward wing,
Hope strips the baffled conqueror of his sting,
The heart communes with spirits from above,
And for a mortal's finds an angel's love;
By wood and stream, where twilight walks beguile,
Hears the soft voice, and sees the undying smile.
He, too, that sorrows for another's woes,
And early dead, the same sad fortune knows,
Hears at the midnight hour the fevered groan,
The cry of mortal pain, the dying moan;
With trembling hand attempts at last to close
The rayless eyes, the lifeless limbs compose,
Sees the brave, gentle bosom fill the grave,
And mourns the son he could have died to save.
To other griefs that changeful life supplies,
Griefs of a race, awakened Memory flies,
And backward as she turns her thoughtful view,
The vanished Indian seems to live anew;
Low voices whisper round from stream and bay,
The mournful tale of nations passed away;
And names, like spirits of the buried race,
Of plaintive sweetness, tell their dwelling-place;
On every isle, in every field and wood,

Shells show, in heaps, where once the wigwam stood;
Spear-points of flint and arrow-heads are found,
Fragments of pottery strew the haunted ground,
And barrows broad, with ancient trees o'erspread,
Still hold the relics of the warrior dead—
Relics of tribes and nations that of yore
Welcomed the Saxon stranger to the shore;
Then masters of the land, with matchless skill,
They chased the deer by valley, plain, and hill,
Through gloomy forests sought a nobler game,
And won, with pride, the warrior's sterner fame;
Where moose and elk their fragrant forest home
In wastes of fir by Madawaska roam;
Where, on his breast, Potomac loves to trace
The patriot's home and hallowed resting place;
In quiet beauty, where Saluda flows;
Catawba rushes from his mountain snows;
Through the lost Eden of the Cherokee,
Where Tallapoosa seeks the Southern sea;
Where slow Oscilla winds his gentler tides,
By cypress shadow where Suwannee glides;
Where, crowned with woods, the Appalachians rise,
The Blue Ridge blends its summit with the skies,
Long rolling waves break foaming from the deep,
And Erie's ocean thunders down the steep;
Lords of the lake, the shore, the stream, the wood,
Painted and plumed, the giant warriors stood,
With presents filled the feeble stranger's hand,
And hailed his coming to the Red Man's land;

Now from these homes expelled, in seeming rest,
A hopeless remnant, cowering in the West,
They linger till the surge of millions come
To sweep them headlong from their transient home;
Vainly the gentle wish, the gen'rous strive
To save the helpless wanderers that survive,
Lure them from sloth, from ignorance and strife,
And make them learn the social arts of life;
In vain, with adverse will, the Indian tries
To win the bread that toil or art supplies,
Like their wild woods before the Saxon's sway,
The native nations wither and decay;
The same their doom where wars the forest sweep,
Like winter torrents rushing to the deep,
Or where the tides of peace more slowly eat
As sure a passage to their last retreat;
Wher'er their lot, with Puritan or Friend,
Friendship and hatred bring one common end;
Chieftain and brave have vanished from the scene,
And memory hardly tells that they have been.
  Such, too, the fate the negro must deplore,
If slavery guard his subject race no more,
If by weak friends or vicious counsels led
To change his blessings for the hireling's bread.
Cheated by idle hopes, he vainly tries
To tempt the fortune that his strength denies,
Quits the safe port, deserts the peaceful shore,
An unknown sea of peril to explore;
Hard the long toil the hireling bread to gain,

Slight is his power life's battle to maintain;
And war's swift sword, or peace, with slow decay,
Must, like the Indian, sweep his race away.
Swift is the doom where temperate climes invite
To fruitful soils the labors of the white;
Where no foul vapor taints the morning air
And bracing frosts his wasted strength repair;
Where Europe's hordes, from home and hunger fled,
Task every nerve and ready art for bread,
Rush to each work, the calls for labor yield,
And bear no sable brother in the field;
There in suburban dens and human sties,
In foul excesses sunk, the negro lies;
A moral pestilence to taint and stain,
His life a curse, his death a social gain,
Debased, despised, the Northern Pariah knows
He shares no good that liberty bestows;
Spurned from her gifts, with each successive year,
In drunken want his numbers disappear.
In tropic climes, where Nature's bounteous hand
Pours ceaseless blessings on the teeming land,
And, with the fruits and flowers that she bestows,
Fierce fevers lurk, the white man's deadliest foes,
More safe the negro seems—his sluggish race
Luxuriates in the hot, congenial place —
A lotus-bearing paradise, that flows
With all the lazy joys the negro knows,
Where all day long, beneath the tamarisk shade,
Stretched on his back, in scanty garb arrayed,

With sated appetite, in sensual ease,
Fanned into slumber by the listless breeze,
A careless life of indolence he lives,
Fed by the fruits perpetual summer gives:
Yet here, unguided by Caucasian skill,
Unurged to labor by a master will,
Abandoned to his native sloth, that knows
No state so blessed as undisturbed repose,
With no restraint that struggling virtue needs,
With every vice that lazy pleasure breeds,
His life to savage indolence he yields,
To weeds and jungle, the deserted fields;
Where once the mansion rose, the garden smiled,
Where art and labor tamed the tropic wild,
Their hard-wrought trophies sink into decay,
The wilderness again resumes its sway,
Rank weeds displace the labors of the spade,
And reptiles crawl where joyous infants played.
Such now the negro's life, such wrecks appear
Of former affluence, industry, and care,
On Hayti's plains, where once her golden stores
Gave their best commerce to the Gallic shores;
While yet no foul revolt or servile strife
Marred the calm tenor of the negro's life,
And lured his mind—with mimicry elate
Of titled nobles and imperial state—
From useful labor, savage wars to wage,
To glut with massacre a demon's rage,
Forget the Christian in the pagan rite,

And serve a negro master for a white.
  But even, in climes like this, a fated power
In patient ambush waits the coming hour,
When to new regions war and want shall drive
Its swarms of hunger from the parent hive,
And Europe's multitudes again demand
Its boundless riches from the willing land
That now, in vain luxuriance, idly lies,
And yields no harvest to the genial skies,
Then shall the ape of empire meet its doom,
Black peer and prince their ancient task resume,
Renounce the mimicries of war and state,
And useful labor strive to emulate.
  Why peril, then, the negro's humble joys,
Why make him free, if freedom but destroys?
Why take him from that lot that now bestows
More than the negro elsewhere ever knows—
Home, clothing, food, light labor, and content,
Childhood in play, and age in quiet spent,
To vex his life with factious strife and broil,
To crush his nature with unwonted toil,
To see him, like the Indian tribes, a prey
To war or peace, destruction or decay?
  Not such his fate Philanthropy replies,
His horoscope is drawn from happier skies;
Bonds soon shall cease to be the negro's lot,
Mere race-distinctions shall be all forgot,
And white and black amalgamating, prove
The charms that Stone admires, of mongrel love,

Erase the lines that erring nature draws
To sever races, and rescind her laws;
Reverse the rule that stupid farmers heed,
And mend the higher by the coarser breed;
Or prove the world's long history false, and find
Wit, wisdom, genius in the negro mind;
If not intended thus, in time, to blend
In one bronze-colored breed, what then the end?
What purposed good, like that which brought before
The Hebrew seer to Nile's mysterious shore,
Brings the dusk children of the burning zone
To toil in fields and forests not their own?
  They come where summer suns intensely blaze,
And Celt and Saxon shun the fatal rays;
Where gay savannas bloom, wild forests rise,
And prairies spread beneath unwholesome skies;
Where Mississippi's broad alluvial lands
Demand the labor of unnumbered hands,
With promised gifts from endless hill and vale,
From fields whose riches mock the traveler's tale,
Where nature blossoms in her tropic pride,
All bounties given, but health alone denied;
They come to cleave the forest from the plain,
From the rank soil to rear the golden grain,
The wealth of hill and valley to disclose,
Make the wild desert blossom as the rose,
To all the world unwonted blessings give,
The naked clothe, and bid the starving live;
Where Amazon's imperial valley lies

Untamed and basking under tropic skies
They come, his secret treasures to unfold—
Spices and silks, and gems and countless gold;
For fields of cane his matted woods displace,
For flocks and herds exchange their reptile race,
With tower and city crown the ocean stream,
And make his valley one Arcadian dream.
Slaves of the plow—when duly tasked they bring,
Like the swart genii of the lamp and ring,
Their priceless gifts—their labors yield in time
Unbounded blessings to their native clime;
Though round it, darkly, clouds and mists have rolled,
Of sloth and ignorance, for years untold,
Still, in the future, Faith's prophetic eye,
Beyond the cloud, discerns the promised sky;
Sees happier lands their sable thousands pour,
Missions of love, on Congo's suppliant shore,
Skilled in each useful civilizing art,
With all the power that knowledge can impart,
O'er the wild deep, whose heaving billows seem
Bridged for their passage by assisting steam,
To Africa, their fatherland, they go,
Law, industry, instruction to bestow;
To pour, from Western skies, religious light,
Drive from each hill or vale its pagan rite,
Teach brutal hordes a nobler life to plan,
And change, at last, the savage to the man.
  Exulting millions, through their native land,
From Gambia's river to Angola's strand,

Where Niger's fountain-head the traveler shuns,
And mountain snows are bright with tropic suns,
See, spreading inward from the Atlantic shore,
Industrial skill and arts unknown before;
Through the broad valleys populous cities rise,
With gilded domes, and spires that court the skies,
Forests, for countless years the tiger's lair,
Yield their glad acres to the shining share;
Where once, along the interminable plain,
The weary traveler dragged his steps with pain,
In iron lines continuous roads proceed,
And steam outstrips the ostrich in its speed;
Timbuctoo's towers and fabled walls, that seem
The fabric only of a traveler's dream,
Spread, a broad mart, where commerce brings her stores
Of gems and gold from earth's remotest shores;
Wealth, art, refinement, follow in her train,
Learning applauds a new Augustan reign,
To tropic suns her fruits and flowers unfold,
And Libya hails, at last, her age of gold.
For these great ends hath Heaven's supreme command
Brought the black savage from his native land,
Trains for each purpose his barbarian mind,
By slavery tamed, enlightened, and refined;
Instructs him, from a master-race, to draw
Wise modes of polity and forms of law,
Imbues his soul with faith, his heart with love,

Shapes all his life by dictates from above,
And, to a grateful world, resolves at last
The puzzling question of all ages past,
Revealing to the Christian's gladdened eyes
How Gospel light may dawn from Libya's skies,
Disperse the mists that darken and deprave,
And shine with power to civilize and save.
Let, then, the master still his course pursue,
"With heart and hope" perform his mission too;
Heaven's ruling power confessed, with patient care
The end subserve, the fitting means prepare,
In faith unshaken guide, restrain, command,
With strong and steady, yet indulgent hand,
Justly, "as in the great Taskmaster's eye,"
His task perform—the negro's wants supply,
The negro's hand to useful arts incline,
His mind enlarge, his moral sense refine,
With Gospel truth his simple heart engage,
To his dull eyes unseal its sacred page,
By gradual steps his feebler nature raise,
Deserve, if not receive, the good man's praise;
The factious knave defy, and meddling fool,
The pulpit brawler and his lawless tool,
Scorn the grave cant, the supercilious sneer,
The mawkish sentiment and maudlin tear,
Assured that God all human power bestows,
Controls its uses, and its purpose knows,
And that each lot on earth to mortals given,
Its duties duly done, is blessed of Heaven.

A SUNDAY MORNING'S DREAM*

From weeks of sickness and the open grave
Saved by His hand whose hand alone can save,
With health returning, in my easy chair
I sat and breathed the balmy summer air,
Through open windows, laden with perfume
Of garden roses in their choicest bloom.
With hope and joy renewed, I gazed around,
Felt a new charm in every sight and sound,
And blest the power that gave for beds of pain
June's fragrant breezes and sweet flowers again.

The Sunday's sky was bright and far and near,
From spire to spire pealed out the call to prayer,
With anxious wish to share its joys once more
I closed my eyes and thought the service o'er;
In fancy saw while listening to its chimes
The ancient tower, the avenue of limes,
The graves adorned with flowers, the cheerful throng,
Organ and choir and books of sacred song,
And parish girls and boys arranged in pairs
The galleries seeking by the spacious stairs.

---

* "Appearance and Reality," a tract by Protestant Episcopal Society, 1857.

I strove to join the throng, the portal gain,
Some influence stopt me and I strove in vain;
When as I stood in wonder fixed and fear
A voice of solemn sweetness reached my ear.
"Mortal, just saved from death, beware," it said;
"Tempt not the second death that waits the dead,
Irreverent long and careless still, deplore
Your heartless worship and offend no more.
Pause, ere in seeming praise you dare again
To mock God's mercy and His house profane;
Pause, ere you desecrate his place of prayer
And for a blessing meet his vengeance there."

As still and mute, in sorrow and surprise
I stood with guilty blush and downcast eyes,
The angel saw and pitied—"Mine the task,"
He said, "to aid what suppliant mortals ask,
To waft their tears, their penitential sighs,
Their grateful prayers, like incense, to the skies;
But ah! how poor the gift the purest give,
How cold the life to God that man can live;
Come, thou shalt see the mockeries of prayer
And learn in time from others to beware;

"Learn that no call by careless lips preferred
For mercy's aid or grace is ever heard.
That when the thoughtless trifler kneels to pray
His words inaudible are swept away,
That even the pious prayer with fervor fraught
To silence sinks, if marred by worldly thought.

Mark, as we enter now, the notes how rare,
How dull, how hushed the sounds of public prayer,
Suppressed the false, irreverent, careless word,
How few, how low, how faint, the voices heard!"

Placed by the altar now, I looked around,
I saw lips moving, but without sound;
I listened for the organ's solemn strain,
The player toiled on but all his toil was vain;
He prest the yielding keys with useless skill,
No sounds sonorous answered at his will;
From the full choir, though straining every throat,
My watchful ear could catch no answering note,
And for the voice of worship long and loud
A dreary silence settled on the crowd.

One voice at last I heard, distinct and clear.
The voice of childhood stole upon my ear,
A voice of prayer like those that cherubs raise,
The voice that God has made perfected praise:
Another too, a broken-hearted cry
For mercy, simply uttered, reached the sky,
Humbly from publican and sinner given—
The angel heard and sped its way to Heaven;
And as he marked the voice, the cry, a smile
Radiant as sunlight flashed along the aisle,
Seraphic rapture shining from his face
Touched every breast and filled the sacred place.

"Search now their hearts and see," the angel said,
"From what foul springs devotion's stream is fed;
The natures see, how tainted and impure,
That Mercy saves and Grace and Love endure;
Judge from their hearts their homage to the skies,
Judge what the gift to God's all-seeing eyes."

At once to higher powers my spirit woke,
My sight grew keener as the angel spoke;
Clear through all hearts I looked and saw within
The serpent forms of every cherished sin,
Envy, a hissing snake, and by its side
Slander of noisome breath and sneering pride,
Ambition, Vanity's fantastic train,
Profusion, and the greedy love of gain;
Deep in the soul concealed the reptile's nest,
Its slimy trail, a glance, a frown, confest,
A scornful smile, a supercilious stare,
An anxious, clouded brow of worldly care,
Titter, and leer, and smirk demure and sly—
Even in the pulpit lurked hypocrisy.

God's house a lair of unclean creatures made,
Half pitying, half indignant, I surveyed,
A cloud of sorrow o'er my spirit hung
And sharp rebukes stood trembling on my tongue.

The angel saw—"You mourn and scorn the scene,"
He said, "Yet such *your* services have been;
Like these *your* heart with passion's breath was stirred,

Like these *your* prayer unworthy to be heard;
Ah! could you witness in the realms above
The depth, the fervor, of Seraphic love.

"Then might you know the mercy that can bear
Your hollow forms and mockery of prayer,
And from the reverent praise of angels know
How poor your heartless service here below.
But mark with care the lesson learned to-day,
For warmer zeal, for holier reverence pray,
Lest from the lesson come a darker doom
And deeper horrors meet you in the tomb."

The voice was still—I, started and amazed,
Around my chamber, half awakened gazed;
The bells were hushed, and in my easy chair
I felt again the balmy summer air,
Through open windows saw the garden bowers
Of vines and roses and its beds of flowers,
And knew that He, supreme and blest, above
Who pours on grateful worlds his gifts of love,
Who late had turned my footsteps from the grave,
Gave too this dream my erring soul to save.
Oh! may the voice of warning sent to chide
My past neglect, my future service guide,
A warmer love, a firmer faith impart,
Shape all my life and purify my heart,
My thoughts, my powers, enlighten and refine
Till Heaven and all its boundless joys be mine.

MARION

I.—THE ESCAPE

The waves grow white, the forest trees
Are bent before the rising breeze;
Sharp lightnings flash, the slanting rain
Courses along the thirsty plain,
Where languid leaf and drooping flower
Rejoicing meet the genial shower;
While blended all the landscape lies
In misty earth and streaming skies;
And startled flock and silent bird,
The shivering horse, the scattered herd,
To fold or copse for shelter flee;
To open shed, or spreading tree.
Yet dauntlessly a tiny sail
Of dingy canvas courts the gale,
And faster hurries, as the mast
Bends lower to the sweeping blast;
And ever, too, the oarsmen ply
Their paddles as the breezes die,
Or flaws in adverse eddies meet,
And strike aback the shivering sheet.

Up Cooper's stream the vessel speeds,
By marshes, flags, and brakes of reeds,
By cypress wood and gloomy pine,

The live-oak and the mantling vine,
The ash and tulip blossomed tree,
The jessamine's wild fragrancy,
And beech, of bark so smooth and fair,
It tempts the hunter posted there,
Or idler's ready knife, to trace
The loved initials on its face.

Still hasting on, the crew invokes
The wind, by Hagan's point of oaks,
And fitfully where breezes blow,
By Strawberry or Pimlico;
They weather Mepkins' marly height,
Pass grove and villa in their flight,
Round Pawley's bend securely wind,
Leave ferry, farm and hall behind.

Yet on, with flowing winds and tides,
From early dawn the shallop glides;
Till now that in the crimson west,
  Enrobed in clouds of gorgeous dyes,
The Sun, departing, sinks to rest,
  With promise of serener skies;
The labor of the day is o'er,
The sharp prow sinks in the shore,
The helmsman, from his weary hand
Casts off the sheet and leaps to land,
And from the awning-place, with care
The sable boatmen gently bear
A pale, disabled Cavalier.

Disabled for the strife of swords,
  He leaves the leaguered town, to find
The rest his forest home affords
  For shattered frame and fretted mind;
Where no unfriendly foot intrudes,
Among his native solitudes,
He seeks the health their scenes supply
Of balmy air and placid sky;
Nursed there by ready hands that gave
Their anxious cares to shield the brave,
With woman's smile to cheer and bless,
Her healing hand of tenderness,
And watchful eye, secure he lies,
Revolves the future enterprise,
And forms, in fancy, for the foe,
The subtle scheme, the sudden blow,
The ambush and the sharp defeat,
The silent march, the sure retreat,
And every keen and crafty plan
That marks the matchless partisan;
While on his couch, in torture tost,
He mourns the venture rashly lost,
The fallen town, the captive host;
And longs for health and strength restored,
To draw again the avenging sword.

For now on Ashley's distant shore,
The din of war is heard no more;
Low lies the patriot's flag, the band

That battled for their native land
On Thaddock's point, a captive host,
No longer guard their country's coast,
Or pent in jail or prison-ship,
With frenzied eye and livid lip,
In fever's wild excitement crave,
And find a refuge in the grave.

Nor was the Briton's fury shown
In cruel wrongs to men alone;
His meaner and unmanly rage
Was wreaked on infancy and age,
With reckless and relentless hand
He gave the homestead to the brand,
And in the homeless child and wife
Made war upon the yeoman's life,
A base, ignoble, brutal strife.

In vain on Camden's luckless plain
Gates tried the chance of war again:
Not his the lot of deathless fame—
The fierce marauding bands to tame,
Repel them from their track of gore
And drive them to their island shore.
Inglorious in the hopeless fight,
Dishonored in the craven flight,
He left DeKalb's great heart to stain
The field with crimson streams in vain.
Stores, cannon lost, a scattered few
Still flying fast where none pursue,

Beneath the fiery August sky
Withered and sere his laurels lie;
And with the luckless Chief's, anew
The country's hopes seem withered too.

II.—THE MUSTER

Who boldly now, with iron will,
  The bloody game yet dare to play?
What noble band, unconquered still,
  Uphold the fortunes of the day?
Not theirs the pomp and proud array
  Of host by king or princes led,
With flaunting plume and banner gay,
  Of silk enwrought with golden thread.

For them no canvas tent is spread,
  Their camp, the tree, the earth, the sky;
The friendly forest gives them bread,
  Their thirst the passing brooks supply.

To distant wood or swamp they hie,
  The secret gathering to meet;
At fortune's call to fight or fly,
  In fiery charge or sure retreat.

With rifle true, on courser fleet,
  What gallant hearts by brake or fen,
Yet quell the foe with daring feat?
  The gallant hearts are Marion's men.

And he, the pale disabled Chief,
 That from the leaguered town afar,
 From din and stir of luckless war,
In solitude had sought relief,
Preserved by Providence to save
A people's cause, and lead the brave,
Who yet unconquered dared oppose
With dauntless heart their country's foes.

Of recent pain the pallid trace
Yet lingered on the leader's face;
But his the air, the martial mien,
The look resolved and yet serene,
In Nature's leader only seen—
His the broad forehead, amply wrought
For miracles of noble thought;
The swarthy cheek and eye of flame,
The active limb and iron frame.*
Invincible to do, or bear
Cold, hunger, toil—in swift career
To charge, with rapid glance to see
And seize the chance of victory;
Or in declining fortune yield,
Yet save the honors of the field;
And merciful as brave, the blow
He warded from the fallen foe,

---

* Though a small man, Marion was invincible to fatigue or exposure.

And nobly scorned in peace to wreak
His country's vengeance on the weak.
He made no wife nor children's need
  The father's evil acts atone,
And lenient to another's deed,
  He craved no grace to shield his own.
Not Arthur's knightly table knew
A knight more loyal, just and true,
Nor Saracen nor Christian bore
A lordlier heart on Syria's shore,
When Cross or Crescent rose or fell,
  As warriors strove to hold or win,
With deeds that minstrels love to tell,
  The holy towers of Saladin;
No Paynim there, nor Templar fought,
Of larger heart or loftier thought.
Amid the country's wreck his star
  Still shone with clear unclouded light,
No mist could hide, nor tempest mar
  The steadfast watcher of the night.
Serene it stood, to mark and cheer
The path in honor's bright career.
And with their Chief, a chosen few,
  That dared the tyrant's rule abhor,
Dauntless, like him, and staunch and true,
  Stood foremost in the ranks of war;

Conyers, the flower of chivalry,
The first to charge, the last to flee;

James, with his sturdy brother band;
Bold Baxter of the iron hand,
And brave Postell, who never knew
Heroic deed too hard to do;
M'Cottry, of unerring aim,
Stern Witherspoon, of giant frame;
McDonald, prompt in every need,
As fiery as his matchless steed;
And skilled alike in feast or fray,
The scout by night, the fight by day,
The rapid march, the patient halt,
The ambush and the bold assault,
Horry, with stammered word, and blow
Like lightning, struck the flying foe.

And many a gallant heart beside,
  The chivalry of Marion's band,
Their Chief's and country's stay and pride,
  When gloom and sorrow filled the land.

What, though the hostile trooper swept,
  To mountain-top from ocean's flood,
And wife and mother raved and wept,
  At daily scenes of tears and blood,
Undaunted still, resolved to dare
  All risk, all loss, with latest breath,
Calmly they trampled on despair,
  Their motto—Liberty or Death—
That once in burning accents broke
  From Henry's lips, when foes amazed

Cried treason, as the speaker spoke,
And startled friends in wonder gazed
That, now, the leader's cap before,
Engraved a silver crescent bore,*
The single emblem, stern and brief,
That spoke the purpose of the Chief.
The summer's anxious sorrows past,
With health restored and hope renewed,
He calls his troop, with bugle blast,
To wage the fierce undying feud;
While life endures, no foe shall stand
Unchallenged on his native land.

October's sky is calm and clear,
The breeze is soft, the balmy air
Steals o'er the senses like a spell,
Where Summer-lingering spirits dwell,
And leave us with a sweet farewell;
Sonorous, then, at early morn,
Is heard the sound of mellow horn;
It dies away, but as it dies,
Another and another rise;
They sweep along the forest side,
Across the river's winding tide,
By swamp and thicket, glade and glen,
The signal horns of Marion's men.

---

* Marion wore on the front of his cap a small silver plate, inscribed with the words "liberty or death," suggested, perhaps, by Henry's famous speech.

Prompt at the call, with fiery speed,
The yeoman mounts his hardy steed.
The saw's rough steel, a scanty store,
Supplies the sword the trooper bore;
The rifle and the hunter's gear,
The arms, the dress, the yeomen wear.
With heart untamed and courage true,
They seek the secret rendezvous,
In dreary swamp and forest, where
  The eagle builds his eyrie nigh;
Far off the timid fold may fear
  The terrors of his beak and eye;
No safety leagues of distance bring;
  With sudden swoop he strikes his prey,
Back to his haunts on rapid wing,
  The bleeding victim bears away.
Here, in their eyrie, watchful, too,
  Bold flights the daring hunters plan,
And far and wide the foe may rue
  The onset of the Partisan;
When mustering fast the yeomen make
The camp fires in the caney brake,
Led by the Chief, whose matchless skill
Held Victory subject to his will.

III.—THE CAMP

On Pee-Dee's swamp, in deep morass,
  'Mid winding creeks and island lies,
Closed every path and secret pass

By tangled woods to prying eyes;
Around in stately columns rise
Huge cypresses, gigantic pine,
Tall oaks that quiver in the skies,
And lither limbs of branching vine;
Grape, twisted supple-jack combine
To spread aloft a leafy maze
So densely, through its arch a line
Of Summer sunlight rarely strays;
Herds there in winter wandering graze
In brakes of cane, so darkly green,
The spotted fawn securely plays,
Protected by the living screen.

Bright plumed, the Summer duck is seen
In hollow oaks, a cunning nest,
And far up earth and sky between,
The heron finds a place of rest.
Here, deep within the silent breast
Of wood and swamp, the leader placed
His secret camp, when sorely prest,
A refuge in a pathless waste.

Of reeds and sod the hunters made
A hamlet in the narrow glade;
Slight shelter, but enough for those
Who love the forest's deep repose,
Its quiet scenes, its simple fare,
Its manly sport, and bracing air.
Around, prepared for all alarms,

Their sylvan armory, their arms,
At easy distance, ready lie
For active hand and watchful eye;
The powder-horn hangs over head,
  On pine or oak the rifle leans,
The hardy horse, in marshes bred,
  His forage there securely gleans;
The smokes of camp-fires to the skies,
  By breath unmoved of passing breeze,
Rose straight and tall, to dreamy eyes,
  Gray trunks of ancient forest trees.
Here scattered yeomen carelessly,
  On gathered leaves, with blanket spread,
  Or long grey moss, a forest bed,
In groups asleep, or resting lie,
Or while away the idle day,
In boisterous sport or quiet play;
Or clean their rifles, and with care
The bullet and the patch prepare;
Or seated by the camp fire boast
  Their gallant deeds of daring done,
When Moultrie kept the island coast,
  And Jasper fame and honors won.

With merry laugh they loved to tell
  Of Ardiesoff's unhappy plight,
When sprawling on the floor he fell,
  His menace turned to sudden fright,

As James with weighty chair replied*
To bullying arrogance and pride.

Of Conyers, too, when hand to hand,
Braving the best of Watson's band,
Daily before the British post
He rode and challenged all their host;—
While in the porch, with taunting mood,
A rebel maid, a captive, stood,
Inviting every foe to try
The freely offered courtesy,
Laughing to see that not a man
Dared meet her rebel partisan.
But most they praised the famous feat
Of James, when on his gallant gray,
Compelled by numbers to retreat,
He held alone the narrow way;
While confident, in full career,
The foe assailed the rebel rear.
There in a road, a fathom wide,
Deep miry swamp on either side,
He singly stood, and dared oppose
The onset of a hundred foes;
With rifle shot and bayonet thrust,
He laid the foremost in the dust;

---

* James had gone into Georgetown, in behalf of his neighbors, to confer with Ardiesoff, commanding the British troops there. The American envoy having been received with insulting menaces, knocked down his opponent with a chair, and made his escape.

Others in quick succession came,
Their charge and luckless fate the same;
Dismay'd, the troop in silence gazed,
And stood admiring and amazed;
Fix'd by some paralyzing charm
To see a single heart and arm,
As with a wizard's potent spell,
The charges of a host repel.

IV.—THE SCOUT

Foremost of all the band to tell
The wild adventures loved so well,
A veteran scout the time beguiles,
With tales of fights and forest wiles;
Of Indian fights and border feuds—
  A veteran scout, but vigorous still
To track, in pathless solitudes,
  Savage, or deer, with matchless skill;
A Pee-Dee man, Old Peter Slade.
Amid the pines' unbroken shade,
By Reedy Creek, his cabin stood,
  Of logs unhewed and daubed with clay;
Around, his pale white-headed brood,
  And grim old dame, at work or play;
While he, unbought by gold or fame,
To fight his country's battles came.
He came in hunting shirt arrayed,
And moccasins of buckskin made,

And coon-skin cap, the brush behind,
To guard his neck from cold or wind:
Smoke-dried, he seemed, with dingy spots
From sooty fires of light wood knots;
Broad-shouldered, wiry, straight and tall,
Ready at race, or wrestler's fall;
His gray eyes twinkled keen and bright,
Like star-eyes in a frosty night;
His ample chest and shaggy head,
And sinewy hand and arm were spread
With coarse strong hair of grizzly red;
His throat with beard or whisker fringed,
His lips and teeth tobacco tinged;
Prompt as a boy at jest or play,
He threw the well-worn quid away,
And by the camp-fire where he lay,
Told the young yeomen gathered round,
  Of many a bloody border strife;
The midnight fire, the captive bound,
  The war-whoop and the reeking knife;
Of scalps in savage triumph spread,
From children torn and woman's head;
Strange, stirring tales, an ample store,
Old stories often heard of yore,
But ever welcome as before.

He told of wars—in martial pride,
  When Grant his Highland heroes led,
And gallantly, and side by side,
  The Briton and Provincial bled;

When promptly, at their chief's command,
Young Marion led the foremost band
Against the ambushed Cherokee;
  Where hidden in the dark ravine
By Shugaw Town or Etchoee,
  The rifle's flash alone was seen,
While the red warrior grimly stood
Concealed amid the gloomy wood,
And sent his messengers of death
In showers upon the foe beneath.
No bolder heart than Marion's there,
Drove the fierce Indian from his lair;
But when the routed braves were driven
  For distant fastnesses to fly,
And stern command by Grant was given
  To burn and waste—no soldier's eye
Like Marion's saw, with pitying tear,
The wigwam blaze, the autumn cheer
Of maize consumed, and savoury bean,
In fields where foot-prints still were seen
Of little children, wont to stray
Among the tassel'd stalks at play,
Whose mothers now in grief and fear
Saw in the waste of battle there,
Famine and sickness and despair.

"You'd not have thought," old Peter said,
  "His heart so soft, with flashing eye,
  And lip compressed and battle-cry,

When in the fierce attack he led,
At Dollard's house, or when he stood
At bay, resolved, by Benbow's wood,
To wait and brave the fierce attack
Of Tarleton's legion on his track."

Now, changed the theme, he told the tale
Of subtle arts that never fail
To hit the Tory's cunning trail,
As surely as the hound pursues
The flying buck through tainted dews.
Boasted how, near the British host,
He shot the sentry at his post;
Or climbing high, or creeping near
In brakes, contrived to see and hear.

He told of marches made by night,
How foes had trembled at their sight,
When in the Tory camp they came,
Like hunter on his midnight game,
That stand with glaring eyes and gaze
Upon the torch's sudden blaze,
Powerless to move, until they fall
Beneath the rifle's fatal ball.

'Twas thus, of late, they found the foe,
  By Nelson's Ford, from Camden's plain,
Advancing carelessly and slow,
  A hundred prisoners in their train.
Fearing no more the rebel crew,

A vanquished, scattered, heartless few,
Prompter to fly than to pursue,
They slumbered idly on the way,
The noontide of an August day;
And little dreamed that Marion's men
Were ambushed in the forest glen—
Waked by the sudden shot, the shout,
The wild huzza, the headlong rout,
Stopt all retreat, no succor nigh,
No chance to fight, or way to fly,
Quickly the luckless Britons learn
How soon the smiles of Fortune turn
To sneering frowns, and sadly yield
The trophies of a happier field.

A young recruit with eager ears*
And heart of fire, the story hears:
Late to the camp the stripling came,
Ardent and emulous of fame—
"And where the men released?" he cried.
  "Snatched from the fate they knew so well,
  The prison ship, a floating hell,
They surely joined our leader's side,
And, eager to wipe out the stain
Of Camden, took the field again!"
"Not so," the cooler scout replied,
"Defeat had crushed their martial pride,

---

* Another James, afterwards Judge James. Six brothers of the name served in Marion's brigade.

No faith had they in Marion's art—
His ready wit and dauntless heart;
They found no stores to tempt them here,
Yielded, like dastards, to despair,
And sought their homes; the men you see
Are those who won the victory."

"Base churls! unworthy to be led
By chief like ours," the stripling said.
"Vile, craven spirits, that could pause
And falter thus in Freedom's cause!—
What next befel? "The maddened foe
Sought vengeance for the daring blow.
Wemys and Tarleton, sent to plan
The ruin of the partisan,
With force and fraud alike essay
To track his steps, to snare his way.
By numbers forced at last to fly,
  Before the storm constrained to bend,
Where Waccamaw's wild sources lie
  The scanty troop of yeomen wend
Their weary way, or, scattered, try
  Their homes and friends to see once more;
Yet ready at the signal cry
  To seek the forest as before.
And soon it came, a flitting bird,
A whistle in the thicket heard,
A distant horn, a long halloo,
Told there was other work to do;

Vengeance for tears from woman wrung,
For homesteads burnt,* for comrades hung,
Like brave Cusack—unheeded there,
And scorned the father's earnest prayer;
The mother kneeled and begged for grace,
They slew the son before her face.
Their ears and eyes were deaf and blind
To gray hairs streaming in the wind,
To cries and shrieks, to frenzy wild,
Of weeping wife and maddened child.
'Twas this, the friend, the captive slain,
The cry for quarter made in vain;
This brought the lion from his den,
This fired the hearts of Marion's men.

"Not vainly shall the injured wait
  For vengeance; with assisting hand
To draw the victim to his fate
Some demon ready seems to stand;
Bide but your time, the fatal power,
  That never mortal step can shun,
Shall bring the inexorable hour
  That wreaks revenge for injuries done.
By Balfour sent to burn and slay
At Tarcote wood new levies lay,
Born to the soil, but now enrolled
And led by Tynes for British gold.
Nor British gold the only cause:

---

* Wemys had great fame as a house-burner.

Some loved their ancient lord and laws,
And, in a nobler spirit, fought
For loftier ends, with purer thought,
Not basely led by lucre bought.
By Tarcote wood secure and gay
They loitered out the roistering day;
Late from the town with loaded train
Of stores, they sought their homes again,
From danger safe—the dreaded foe
To distant wilds compelled to go,
Or scattered round, an easy prey,
Their watchful leader far away.
In wassail deep the day is spent,
On wild carouse and revel bent,
They dance and reel, the night prolong
With cards and dice, with jest and song;
Some slumber by the forest side,
Some tell their boasted deeds, and lied.
The present safe, the future bright,
Away all thought of ills to-night!
'Drink to the king, and damn the cause
Of traitors that oppose his laws!'
So shouted Campbell, of the band
The fiercest heart, the bloodiest hand.
'No need' he cried, 'with us, for care,
Let Marion's followers think of fear;
Curse on his cunning, may the rope
And hangman prove his only hope;

Curse on the ragged, rebel crew,
The halter be their portion too;
Huzza for George!'—'twas hardly said,
A bullet, from the thicket sped,
Struck in his boast the boaster dead.
And bursting on the startled ear,
The tramp of horsemen thundered near.
Up to their feet the revellers sprung,
Down cup and can and flagon flung;
Then rose upon the startled ear
The scream of terror and despair,
Half waked the dizzy sleepers reel
Beneath the charger's iron heel,
The rifle in the darkness flashed,
Through crouching crowds the trooper dashed—
All thought of battle laid aside,
Wings to the flying fear supplied.
But Tarcote Swamp is deep and drear,
The night was dark, the refuge near,
The scattered bands found shelter there.
Off with the dawn of morning light
  The sleepless Chief unwearied flew;
He never lingered to invite
  Surprise, nor paused if aught to do
Remained undone—new foes to meet,
  With ready arm and judgment true,
Again, on coursers sure and fleet,
  He led the stern, determined few;
Nor night from day their service knew,

All times alike—attack, retreat,
Their ready steps where duty drew,
The rapid onset they repeat.
They kept no road nor beaten path,
They sought no bridge on passing stream,
They swam the river in his wrath,
They came, they vanished, like a dream;
Unlooked-for, like the sudden flash
Of summer lightning, and their blow,
Terrific as the thunder crash,
With fear and wonder struck the foe.
With them no flaunting pennon waved,
No cannon lumbering shook the ground,
No trumpet when the battle raved
Or paused, retreat or onset sound;
But silent, like a sprite, they came,
The rifle's flash proclaimed them near,
They swept along like sudden flame
Through forests in the early year.
In march or charge, in field or flood,
Ford, deeper river, still alone
He ever led, he spared the blood
Of all, unsparing of his own.
Vain was the Briton's boasted claim
To conquest, vain the blood it cost,
The unconquered soul remains the same—
While that endures no cause is lost;
It yields while foes too strong prevail,
Resumes the conflict as before,

As saplings bend before the gale,
Erect and strong the tempest o'er."

"What glorious sport!" with flashing eyes
And flushing cheeks, the youth replies;
"But tell me of the conflict, when
With twenty picked of Marion's men*—
With twenty matched, in open field,
You forced the enemy to yield.
Which are the gallant men you chose
To meet the challenge of your foes?"
"One near, with busy hands you see,
Cleaning the rifle on his knee;
Broad-chested, like a bull, his hair,
Black, glossy, like an autumn bear;
A bolder heart or stronger hand
Rode never yet in Marion's band.
Another leans on yonder bay,
In hunting shirt and leggings gray,
With folded arms and hunter's eye,
Watching the wild ducks whizzing by;
Straight as a sapling, strong and tall,
And apt alike, in festive hall,
In dance, or danger's sudden call.
Another by the camp-fire stands,
Busy among the blazing brands;

---

* His opponents complained that Marion relied on stratagem and surprise, and challenged his troop to a contest of twenty picked men, in open field.

Some dainty for his dinner there,
The product of his trap or snare,
Squirrel or rabbit, asks his care;
A raw-boned, iron man, his frame
Nor time can bend, nor labors tame;
No scout like him! By night, by day,
He tracks the deer or foeman's way;
No quicker eye, no surer aim,
For battle-field or forest game.
Vanderhorst their leader, on they went,*
  To meet the challenge of the foe.
No guests on feast or wedding bent
  With lighter step or spirits go.
The field at hand, with sudden cheer
They forward rush—the place is bare,
On silent wing the bird is flown,
Brave McIlraith has wiser grown;
Withdraws his chosen men and flies,
  Rushes from wood to wood, and foils,
  By rapid march, the hunter's toils,
And—lost his laurels—gladly tries
In distant garrison to meet
The triumph of a safe retreat."

V.—THE FLAG

The story paused, but forward bent,
  The listeners, with insatiate ear,

* Pronounced Vandross.

Sat all unwearied, and intent
  Some other gallant deed to hear.
But most the tale of war inflames
The brother of the veteran James,
The lad whose questions brief and bold,
His frank and ardent spirit told;
New to the war, he longed to try
His skill and strength of arm and eye;
For often in the forest near
His shot had stopped the bounding deer,
And rapid as the flash of light
Had struck the partridge in her flight.

But mute the wily hunter lies,
And peers around with searching eyes
And frowning brow. His ready ear
Had caught the sound of footsteps near;
And soon the parted boughs between
Two scouts of Marion's band are seen;
Between the two, with bandaged eyes,
To guard their fastness from surprise,
In scarlet dress a third appears.
A flag of truce the Briton bears—
He comes commissioned to provide
  Exchange of prisoners, and to frame
Some plan, to curb on either side,
  The license that disgraced its name;
To crush the base marauding bands
  That marred the noble soldier's toils,

The bandit hordes, whose felon hands
  With murder reeked and bloody spoils.

With calm, frank air, and courteous word,
  The forest warrior met his guest,
The plan with glad attention heard,
  The wish with earnest warmth exprest
That something they might do to stay
The license of that bloody day.
Brave hearts with equal honor fraught,
Soldiers alike in deed and thought,
Each, in his foe, with ready eyes
A brother seemed to recognize.

The business done, and noon-day near,
  The parting guest was prest to stay:
"Stop," said the Chief, "my larder share;
  'Tis ampler than is wont, to-day;
Whatever be the dish, at least,
You're warmly welcomed to the feast."

They sat, the chair a fallen pine,
  Its bark their dish; the simple fare
Potatoes, and the daintiest wine—
  Cool water from the fountain near.
With wonder struck, the Briton viewed
The drink, the furniture, the food:
"Is this your life," he gravely said,
"Is this your daily meat and bread?
On food like this, will soldiers stay,

To watch by night, to fight by day,
And give their blood and lives away?"
"We fight for freedom, not for pride,
Or wealth, or power," the Chief replied.
The Briton bowed—his manly heart
  Was moved—in silence on his way,
Thoughtful he went. "Is mine the part
  To fight such men," he said, "for pay?
No never!" To his island shore
  He turned his steps, his sword resigned,
Untainted with fraternal gore.
  He left no nobler heart behind.
How few like him! how few that give
  The dismal tales of every clime
A brighter page, and nobly live
  To cheer the waste of wrong and crime;
Tales else that hatred and disgust
Would spurn and trample in the dust.

Rare are the noble hearts that, strong
  In fixt resolve and purpose high,
Retain amid the common throng
  Some semblance of their native sky;
Not theirs the part, with groveling eye,
  To watch Ambition's paths alone,
And every mean allurement try
  To make her maddening heights their own.
With hand of steel, with heart of stone,
  Not theirs through carnage to obtain

The victor's wreath, the monarch's throne,
  And deluge earth with crimson rain;
Nor theirs, the deep enduring stain
  Of those that, formed for nobler aim,
For truth, for honor, basely train
  Their powers to grope for party fame,
To win from fools or knaves a name—
  To worship Mammon, to degrade,
For office sake, the sacred flame
  By Heaven for nobler objects made;
The flowers of genius shrink and fade—
  Even they shall moulder into dust,
If on unhallowed altars laid
  To wreathe the brows of wine or lust:
Time with no laurel crowns the bust
  Of him who basely trades away
His birthright and the sacred trust,
  For the low purpose dares betray,
To him the garlands of a day;
  Not those of amaranth belong,
Such as diviner brows display,
  That love the right and scorn the wrong:
Alas! that, lost amid the throng,
  His name unpraised we never knew,
To whom applause and minstrel song,
  Love, honor, monuments are due;
His name, who bravely cast aside
Advancement, friendship, martial pride,

And scorned the efforts to enslave,
By arms, the noble and the brave.

VI.—THE ALARM

Dark shadows rest on field and wood;
  No ray of star or moon's dim light
Pierces the murky mists that brood
  On swamp and stream—a double night;
Still all—save when at times is heard
  An insect's chirp, a sudden neigh,
The flitting of a startled bird,
  The owl cry, prowling after prey;
Dimly the camp-fires wear away,
  Then, startlingly, with transient glare,
Blaze brightly out in seeming play;
  Around deep gloomy caves appear,
Black, limitless, and from the ground,
With trailing vines, like serpents bound,
Trees, like huge columns, start, and then
Sink down at once to earth again.

But now, amid the camp, the stir
  Of action breaks the hush of night:
Abrupt and hurried, like the whirr
  Of partridge roused to hasty flight;
They're off—before the paling ray
Of moonlight brightens into day,
The distant loyalist shall know
And rue the vigor of their blow—

When Ganey, Barfield, trembling hear,
From rifle shot and charging cheer,
The dreaded partisan is near.

His scouts out-lying, far and wide,
Each hostile post and fort beside,
Were come to tell, the gathering foe—
Watson above and Doyle below,
Had marched to strike some secret blow—
That many a Tory troop had sped
  With Richbourg, from their distant post;*
That Harrison his people led
  To swell the Briton's growing host;
They march to break the secret charm,
  The hidden spell that seemed to lie
In Maham's potent sword and arm,
  That flashed from Marion's eagle eye,
  A light that led to victory.

To take his island camp, they thought,
  Would stain the leader's spotless fame,
And mar the magic gift that brought
  Such boundless power to Marion's name.
Fools!—'t was the soul that gave the eye
And hand their ready mastery;
With it, what daring deeds are wrought,
What trophies won, what battles fought,

* Celebrated Tory leaders.

From countless hosts what victories won,
Like Salamis and Marathon;
Without it, walls of brass impart
No courage to the craven heart;
Not miry swamp, nor secret glen—
Souls were the forts of Marion's men.

On every side his scouts recall
  His distant parties from their post,
In one strong band he gathers all
  To hurl them on the hostile host;
Prompt to anticipate the blow,
He rushes on the nearest foe.

A thousand men by Watson led,
  With steady tramp and spirits gay,
March gallantly, their banners spread,
  A regiment in proud array,
And Richbourg's troopers in the van,
  Keen woodsmen all, with practiced eyes,
Glen, thicket, brake, with caution scan,
  To guard them from the foe's surprise.
But soon the empty saddles show
The presence of their active foe;
The bullet flies from every wood,
The scarlet coat is died in blood.
With riflemen the forest swarms,
The swamp 's astir with flitting forms;

On every side, flank, front and rear,
They charge, recede, and re-appear;
No pause, no respite, soon and late,
The bullet whizzes, winged by fate;
Despondingly, his vaunting gone,
The weary Briton hurries on.
The river near, his hope revives,
To reach its friendly bank he strives;
Across, his panting troops may meet
A resting place for weary feet.
The hope is vain, the bridge is fired,
  The plank removed; no passage there
Awaits the Briton, faint and tired,
  The day far spent and Marion near.

Beyond the bridge, the river nigh,
  By trees concealed, in wood or fen,
M'Cottrey's longest rifles lie,
  The sharpest shots of Marion's men.
Upon the adverse bank, in vain,
  High overhead, with ceaseless roar,
From brazen mouths, their iron rain
  The British cannon idly pour;
Safe, from his tree, the hunter's eye
And ringing rifle shot reply—
And headlong, like the forest game,
The Briton sinks beneath his aim.
He falls, but promptly of his band,
Another takes the staff and stand;

Before the rifle's deadly ball
Another and another fall:
No private dares, at last, to face
The terrors of the fatal place;
But gallantly their chief assumes
The dreaded risk—his nodding plumes
Attract a hundred vengeful eyes—
In blood the daring leader lies;
Then rushing where the bodies lay
His friends would bear the corpse away:
Vain the attempt—the bullet speeds,
Beside the dead the rescuer bleeds;
And Watson sees, with wild despair,
The helpless, hopeless slaughter there;
Back to his fortress gladly flies,
And curses, with reverted eyes,
The foe and fatal enterprise.

Then, like a lion to his lair
  That bears and wolves had dared to waste,
Too late to save, but to repair
  And to avenge, the hunters haste;
Doyle's Tory scouts had learned to trace
The pathways to the secret place.
His troop had seized its meagre spoils,
The gathering of the hunter's toils;
Then, frightened at their work, in dread
To meet the coming vengeance fled:

In vain—no speed, no arts avail
  To save them from the avenging foe;
Horry and Maham track their trail
  As wolves the wounded buffalo,
When bleeding on the grassy plain
The prairie monarch tries in vain
To fly—the fierce, insatiate gang
Around his weary quarters hang,
Grow bolder with his failing breath,
And drag the giant to his death;
So fast the panting Briton flew,
So fierce his eager foes pursue;
Arms, knapsack, canteen, cast aside—
No season this for martial pride,
Not fame the end, the desperate strife
Is waged on either side for life:
To take, to save, the peril past,
The flying squadrons pause at last,
And Camden, in her distant post,
Gives safety to the routed host.

VII.—THE CHANGE

Fortune, that with capricious smile
  Lures and deludes the eager throng,
Most loves the wary to beguile:
To bend the proud, to break the strong;
And now in her accustomed way,
  With frowns for smiles, she turns to meet

The Briton's insolence of sway,
  And change his triumph to defeat;
Ebbs the full tide, the crimson flush
  Of conquest sinks in deepening gloom,
From vale and glen, the swelling rush
  Of numbers tells his coming doom;
Sumter's indomitable will,
And Pickens with adroiter skill
Their fiery followers lead again
To sweep the posts of hill and plain;
And Greene, his country's sword and shield,
  With troops now trained to war's array,
Hurries from Guilford's bloody field
  To drive the leopard from his prey:
He comes—the foe no longer dares
  His wasted squadrons to divide,
But from each distant post prepares
  To draw his forces to his side.
Now far and near, with slackened rein,
Shall Marion's troopers scour the plain,
From golden fields of Waccanaw,
  To where in wider circuit flow
  The southern floods of Edisto,
His sword is government and law;
He sweeps the country from the main
Like autumn storms of wind and rain;
Post, fortress, vainly strive to stay
Or fetter his resistless way,
And check the fortunes of the day.

Fort Watson, from its lofty site,
  Defiance dared, but dares no more;
From logs built up to loftier height
  Their deadly shot the yeomen pour,
So sharp, so true; the work is done,
The banner struck, the fortress won,
And vain for succor or relief
The message to their distant chief.
'Twas then the patriot matron gave
  Her stately mansion to the flame;
She saw, to save it, was to save
  The hostile fort that bore her name.
With generous haste, that scorned to pause
In honor's and her country's cause,
She lent the flaming shaft that flew
  The bow that winged its way on high,
And calmly stood and smiled to view
  Her cherished home in ashes lie.
While fashion's idle votaries die
  Unknown, the insects of a day,
The light of immortality
  Around her brow shall ever play;
In poet's tale, in minstrel's lay,
  The deed shall never be forgot,
And history's pages shall display,
  For aye, the gentle name of Motte.
In maiden's song it finds a place,
Its sweetest ornament and grace;

On every tongue, a household word,
That honored name is ever heard.
Taught by devotion pure and warm
  Like this, each manly bosom glows,
It lends his cause a brighter charm,
  It gives new force to Freedom's blows;
Resistless now her arms shall sweep
The proud invader to the deep.

No more shall Carolina lie
Prostrate in mortal agony,
No longer shall her valleys feel
The accursed tramp of hostile heel,
Nor, day by day, shall field or flood
Be stained with streams of native blood;
But ever on, her foot shall climb
The heights of fame to endless time,
And trophies won in war or peace
By gallant sons, shall never cease.

Bright as thy skies, my native land,
  In glory's path thy steps shall shine.
No braver heart nor readier hand,
  At honor's call, shall come than thine.
Where fight the foremost, ever there
  Thy sword shall cross the haughtiest foe;
No flag in victory's proud career
  A nobler place than thine shall know.
No eloquence in Senate hall,

Of bolder tone or loftier flight,
Shall crush the false, the base appall,
Uphold and vindicate the right.
By Freedom's arc and altar, none
Keep watch and ward with keener eye,
With deeper scorn, the traitor shun,
Clear in their hallowed ministry.

Nor yet has earth's supremest race
Borne forms and faces more divine
In virgin loveliness and grace,
More soft, more bright, more pure than thine;
The gifts, sweet look, sweet speech, sweet thought,
The maiden gifts of Chaucer's lay,
None live of earth more richly fraught
With all these gentle gifts than they.
So ever onward be thy course,
So brave thy sons, thy daughters chaste,
And never be by fraud or force
Thy honors stained, thy arms defaced.
Proudly, with flashing eye of scorn,
Look down, if slander dare defame,
No lying tongue of woman born
Shall taint the lustre of thy name:
Too high, too bright, thy glorious sphere
For carrion birds to shelter there.

VIII.—EUTAW

September's sky is calm and clear,
A vault of fire—the burning air*
An oven's breath; the wasted rill
Sinks and deserts the idle mill;
The reservoir is dry, its bed
A pasture with rank grasses spread;
The sluggish cattle in the shade
Chew lazily; the shriveled blade
Of grass or maize is crisp and sere,
Dews fall no more; the mid-day glare
Is blinding—birds have ceased to sing,
The crow alone is on the wing,
With piercing eye and subtle scent
And mustering caw, on plunder bent;
The breath of every breeze is lost,
The lightest feather upward tost
Sinks down to earth; on lake or stream
No ripple breaks the dazzling gleam;
A quivering haze is on the ground,
A death-like quiet slumbers round:
When suddenly a sound of fear
Roars on the forest's startled ear—
The rush of war, the iron heel
Of horse, the clang of hostile steel,
The tramp of men, the solemn boom
Of cannon shot, a voice of doom.

*** The battle was fought on an intensely hot day of September.**

Greene, like an eagle from his rock,
  His wings new plumed, his force restored,
Swoops down upon the frightened flock,
  From Santee's hills, by Howel's ford.
Not burning suns can stop his way,
Nor fever hosts of summer stay,
Nor troops, nor stores withheld, delay
His onward course—from short repose
He rushes on his slumbering foes.
And foremost there the task to share,
The conflict meet, the peril dare,
Are Marion's men; no keener eye,
No bolder heart to do or die
Greene's steadiest veterans supply.

Where Eutaw's fountains, deep and clear,
  Pour out at once a river's force,
  A thicket fringing all its course,
An open field and mansion near,
The battle raged—a fiercer strife,
More prodigal of blood and life,
Fought never Rome's resistless bands,
  When, yet their vigor fresh and young,
  On conquering wings their eagles hung,
O'er African or Asian lands.

Beneath the lofty, leafy arch,
  Within the grand primeval shade
Of forest trees, their adverse march,
  On either side, the armies made;

And now their chiefs with skill and care
The frowning front of war prepare;
Malmedy, Marion, Pickens, form
  The foremost line; their yeomen meet
The first, fierce fury of the storm,
  Its iron hail and fiery sleet;
Next, stately, like a towering oak,
  Campbell arrays his martial train
From distant Dan and Roanoke,
  From mountain ridge and piny plain;
Beside them Williams, true and tried,
Hardman and Howard by his side,
Ranges his band, Patapsco's pride;
And gaily Kirkwood's Delawares
  Their post assume—a host, though few,
When war his sternest aspect rears
  No braver heart, nor hand more true,
  The sword of battle ever drew.

Bold, too, and firm the hostile ranks—
  Stewart, like a Briton, scorns retreat,
And Coffin and Majoribanks*
  Are worthy of the foes they meet.

In quiet woods that ne'er before
Had echoed to the battle's roar,
Where lowing herds alone were heard,
Or warbled song of hidden bird,
The conflict raves—the trembling ground,

* The name is given as spelt, not as pronounced.

With bursting shell or crashing ball,
Is rent and torn, from trees around
The shattered leaves and branches fall;
Fiercer the roar of battle grows,
With roll of drum and furious shout,
And teeth firm set and flashing eye,
And leveled steel, resistlessly,
They charge, the clashing bayonets close;
A moment's pause of anxious doubt,
A moment's pause, then fiercely on,
Like torrent, bank and barrier gone,
Williams and Campbell sweep the field,
Like lurid clouds that break and fly,
Before the gale, along the sky,
The hostile bands disordered yield;
The day is won!—but, ah, how soon
May Fortune's frown her gifts resume—
Snatch from the hand her brightest boon,
And turn the sunlight into gloom.
In vain achieved the glorious deed,
For honor and their country's need,
Still many a gallant heart must bleed.

The strong-walled mansion-house behind,
The flying host a fortress find,
And tents invitingly are near,
And tables with abundant cheer,*

---

* The British tents were standing, and tables spread with refreshments for the troops, when the Americans reached them.

To half-fed troops a tempting snare;
Alas! that Victory's foot should pause
And falter for so light a cause,
Losing the precious moment when,
  The chance once lost, no more success
  Returns with smiling lip to bless
The fleeting hopes of mortal men.
'Tis lost, the rallying foes reform
  Their broken ranks with small delay;
Vainly may Campbell toil to storm
  The mansion fort that bars his way;
Idly, a prodigal of life,
He dares the charge with peril rife
And sinks amid the unequal strife.
And vainly Washington assails
  The band that held the British flank
  In copses hid by Eutaw's bank;
Fierce though the charge, the onset fails,
'Mid stunted oaks and saplings, where
  Majoribanks still kept his post
Like Paladin that knew no fear;
  The charger falls—the rider's lost—
A prisoner on the battle field,
Wounded, entangled, forced to yield
The sword he could no longer wield.
He sinks, the flag that ever flew
  Foremost, where peril called the brave,
Then first the freaks of fortune knew,
  And sunk beneath the crimson wave

Of battle; vainly now to save
His comrade, Hammond cuts his way;
Blackened with powder, stained with blood,
He strives to pierce the firm array,
In vain, that still undaunted stood
Protected by the pathless wood.

With ready hand and practiced eye,
Had Marion and his men been nigh
To force the covert foes to yield
The wood, and take the open field,
And give the trooper's sabre room,
Far different then had been the doom
Of him whose sword's resistless sway
Had shorn the crest of Tarleton's pride,*
And turned, on Guilford's bloody day,
With Gunby's charge, the battle's tide.†

The baffled troops, at last, retire;
Greene stays their onset and recalls,
He sees their ineffectual fire
Is vainly poured on solid walls;
And useless charge his troopers make
On pathless copse and tangled brake.
Another fierce September sun
Must close the work so well begun,

* At the Cowpens.

† The charge of Gunby's regiment and Washington's cavalry decided the day at Guilford Court-House.

And, restlessly, with hope elate,
The morrow's call the hunters wait,
To drive the quarry to his fate.

But long before the morrow's dawn
The tents are struck, the foe is gone,
Arms, wounded, stores abandoned, fast
  And far, before the morning's light
  Shall tell the beaten Briton's flight.
He hastes away—the peril's past—
Yet, as he flies, among the trees
The deadly rifleman he sees;
In every copse and swamp and fen,
He dreads the shot of Marion's men,
Till panting, through the sun, he finds
His safety in the city lines.

IX.—PEACE

The toilsome task at last is done,
The battle fought, the victory won;
Far through the land the cheering light
  Of peace, with welcome radiance gilds
The lowliest vale, the loftiest height,
  The cot, the hall, with rapture fills;
Matron and maid alike rejoice,
Gray-headed seniors and their boys,
The widow's heart forgets its pain—
The lost has not been lost in vain,
And Peace may fill his place again:
The mother, of her sons bereaved,

Though nothing earthly gives relief,
In freedom for their home achieved
Yet finds a balm that soothes her grief.
No lot so low but sees a bliss
In Peace and Hope's fair promises.

And what of those who fought and bled,
With constancy almost divine,
Whose toil and blood for years had fed
The feeble fire on Freedom's shrine;
Of those whose iron nerve had rent
The chain that bound the timid crowd,
Whose hearts by adverse years unbent,
To Fortune's power had never bowed:
The ragged soldier—what of him?
Do open hands their gifts bestow—
Do hearts with generous ardor glow—
Honoring the mutilated limb,
The gaunt, scarred frame? With garlands bound,
Praised, petted, followed, flattered, crowned;
March-worn and labor-wasted now,
Unfit for toil of spade and plough;
Finds he at last some happier lot,
Some nook of ease and bounteous cheer?
His wounds and sufferings are forgot,
His claims excite a smile or sneer,
Disbanded, scattered to the winds,
No place of rest the veteran finds;

A burthen to his country grown,
  Compelled to beg or take his bread;
No cur, that gnaws his lonely bone,
  More grudgingly was ever fed.
Upon that bright December day,
When crowded transports filled the bay
To bear the conquered hosts away,
The common joy had been complete
  If, while the favoring breezes blew,
The bay had borne another fleet
  Of transports for the conquerors, too;
Fond wishes, then, for favoring gales
Had filled the soldier's parting sails;
Warm hopes had moved the people's heart
  That Fortune, with auspicious hand,
  Would lead to some far richer land
The veteran, and would there impart
Her amplest, fairest gifts, that they
  The burthen might no longer bear;
Now hateful grown, of food or pay,
  For war, a foe no longer near;
The debt of gratitude too great,
They left the soldier to his fate.

Yet, though the many spurned his claim,
And scorned the warrior's honest fame,
All generous hearts—a noble few,
  Amid the base more purely bright,
As beacon lights that, ever true,

Shine clearest in the darkest night —
All generous hearts, with grief, deplore
The war-worn soldier's scanty store,
The country's promise falsely spoken,
The contract made and meanly broken;
The garb of rags, the dole of food,
The country's base ingratitude;
And gentler hearts with pity glow,
And favors fairer hands bestow,
And love's sweet sympathies impart
Their treasure to the veteran's heart;
His toils reward, his fortunes cheer—
Who more than he deserves the fair?

For him, the bravest of the brave,
Who, in his country's darkest hour,
Still bade her dauntless banner wave,
And spurn the stern invader's power;
For him one gentle bosom warmed,
One eager ear, intent to hear,
Insatiate sought the tale that charmed
Her heart with Marion's great career:
She loved the high heroic name,
The courage, ever prompt to dare,
The Patriot Chief's unspotted fame,
The gentle spirit, prone to spare,
That through long years of civil strife
With wrong and rancorous passions rife
Had passed without reproach or fear;

And now could challenge friend or foe,
In all that brave and bright career,
One blot or stain or shade to show,
Conscious no tongue of truth could speak
A charge to flush his manly cheek.

Her warm devotion, many a day,
Had smoothed and cheered the warrior's way,
The wanted aid had ever lent
The secret message often sent,
To warn him of the cunning wile,
The Briton's wrath, the Tory's guile;
And, now, his suit the warrior pays,
Nor pays in vain—she loved to praise
The chief and matchless partisan;
And from the chief to love the man
Is but an easy step, 'tis said,
Though silver threads, not singly now,
About the wooer's temple spread,
And broader showed his noble brow;
But still, in minstrel's tale, 'tis sung,
That heartfelt love is ever young,
Nor ceases with his purest light,
With tenderness as warm as true,
In winter climes to shine as bright
As spring or summer ever knew.

X.—RETIREMENT

Sweet is repose by labor earned,
  And safety won from perils past,
As skies, through breaking clouds discerned,
  Are brightened by the stormy blast,
And smile upon the gazer's sight
With softer blue in purer light.
Amid his old ancestral woods,
  The forest pines, that sentries stand,
  Like marshalled giants of the land,
To guard its solemn solitudes,
The mansion-house of Marion rose,
  With peace, and love, and honor blest,
Of weary wars a fitting close;
  A place of joy, a home of rest,
A shrine of hospitality.
Its open portals sought the eye
  Of every stranger wandering by,
And with a welcome, sure and warm,
  Enticed his lingering step to stay,
And won him, with a growing charm,
  To loiter joyous weeks away;
Around the board, of ample cheer,
  With hearts still young, from day to day,
The veteran warriors revelled there;
  Alert and strong, though worn and gray,
And listened with unwearied ear,
  Or talked of battles fought and won;

And sometimes with a soldier's tear,
  They named the names of comrades gone—
Brave hearts, but fated not to see
Their country's final victory.

On either side the mansion lay
  Broad pastures for the generous steed,
There petted colts at pleasure play,
  And flocks and herds securely feed;
With bell adorned, about the lawn,
  Of lustrous eye and agile limb,
A deer half tamed, a forest fawn,
  Walks gently or, in sudden whim
Or causeless fright, with graceful bounds,
Leaps the high fence and scours the grounds;
So lightly, airily it springs,
The creature seems to move on wings.

More distant field and swamp sustain
A varied crop of golden grain,
And ample barns, with open door,
Welcome the rich autumnal store;
To help the hospitable fare,
The ready forest gives its share:
Fat turkeys first—the table's pride—
The partridge pasty by their side;
Blue teel and summer ducks supply
Another faultless luxury;
And rice-reared birds—more delicate
A dainty princess never ate:

The lake, the pond, their daily dish
And sport bestow, of various fish,
The choicest product of the stream,
Delicious trout and peerless bream.
But chiefest of the country cheer,
Plump haunches of the forest deer—
Not like the park's that, fed and tame,
Can give no taste to sylvan game:
These range at will the distant woods,
And browse the glades and swim the floods;
And, when the hunter's horn is heard,
  And opening dogs are on the cry,
No sport so deeply ever stirred
  The heart with joy. The hunter's eye
Flashes with fire, he spurs his steed
Through bush and brake with furious speed,
Till reached the stand, his steady aim
And sharp shot stop the flying game.
Brave sports, and worthy to impart
Due vigor to the hand and heart,
To train them for the bolder game
That guards their country's flag and fame;
Who that has felt the joy it gives,
But loves the life the hunter lives,
When free as air he wildly roves
The hill, the vale, the fields and groves;
Where nerve and eye, from every scene,
Fatigue and toil, grow strong and keen;
Fit, too, the sport for veterans, when

The bolder hunting past of men—
They want some mimic scene of strife
To mind them of their ancient life.

Here, prompt to do each generous deed,
The widow help, the orphan feed,
With ready hand and open door,
To right the wronged, to aid the poor:
In every plan for good to lead,
To give desert its fitting meed.
Truth, knowledge, virtue to sustain,
The jars of new-made peace restrain
With vigorous hand and steady rein,
He lived beloved—his waning years
  Flowed softly as a river flows,
  Where green and flowery banks enclose
A quiet stream that gently bears
Its tribute to the parent deep,
And in its bosom sinks to sleep.

Sleep, gallant warrior, calmly sleep!
  No mummeries shall here presume,
With heartless pageantries to heap
  And desecrate thy simple tomb;
To virtue reared with reverent care,
  By Love and Truth alone adorned,
No false pretense has offered there
  The homage by thy spirit scorned;
It stands thy woodland home beside,
  Where Eutaw's storied waters flow;

It needs no gift of pomp or pride,
  Of vanity or vulgar show.
Fitly the forest warrior lies
  In groves with mossy draperies hung,
His dome of state the vaulted skies,
  By birds his requiem daily sung:
The wild deer bounds and browses near,
  Around it sated herds repose,
And on his sculptured name the year
  Drops crimson leaf-showers at its close.
Fair, like the scene, thy deed and thought
  The pure example ever finds,
With nature's blended influence fraught
  Apt audience here with noble minds.
Long ages hence, the voice of fame
  Shall love its lessons to prolong;
Long ages hence, thy cherished name
  Shall live the light of tale and song:
A light, a lustrous star, beside
  The radiant host that shine to cheer
Ingenuous hearts, and prompt and guide
  Their course in honor's high career.
Sleep, gallant chief, around thy grave
  No sculptured busts nor columns rise,
But hither come the fair, the brave,
  With swelling hearts and brimming eyes,
And feel, as at some hallowed shrine,
An influence here almost divine.

THE LAMENT OF FEZZAN FOR HER CHIEF

Denham and Clapperton, when in Africa, set out from Moorzuk under the protection of Boo Kaloom, a Fezzan chief of great distinction, who had been persuaded to join the Sultan's troops in an incursion into the Fellatah country. Unsupported by his allies, who ran away at the first difficulty, the Arab sword and gun proving to be no match for the spears and poisoned arrows of the Fellatahs, Boo Kaloom was killed with a great number of his Arabs. Denham had a narrow escape. On the return of the survivors to Fezzan, the women lamented their chief with songs of praise and mourning for many days.

Trust not the sword nor faithless gun,
But let the boldest shrink with fear
When Boo Kaloom, the brave and good,
Falls by the unbeliever's spear.

Like the broad moon among the stars,
The chief of Fezzan matchless shone;
Where now shall Fezzan look for aid,
That rested on his aid alone?

Low lies the shepherd of his flock—
Low lies the pride of Arab lands—
Let men with sorrow hang their heads,
Let women wring their helpless hands.

Mourn him with praises and with song,
  Yet who can hope his praise to tell,
Whose heart was like the desert large,
  And bounteous as the desert well,

Or as the camel's milky stores
  From Fezzan's palmy plains, that give
New vigor to the sinking troop,
  And bid the fainting traveler live?

As droop the flowers when rains are passed,
  Droops Moorzuk, mourning for the slain,
Pierced by the heathen's poisoned shaft,
  Stripped on the heathen's distant plain.

Parched now by burning sands and sun,
  Swept now by chilling winds of night,
The arm that gave his people strength,
  The eye that gave his people light.

Oh trust not sword nor faithless gun,
  But let the boldest shrink with fear,
When Boo Kaloom, the brave and good,
  Falls by the unbeliever's spear.

THREESCORE YEARS AND SEVEN

Life's voyage, by rock and shoal, is near its close,
The billow buffeted, the gale endured;
Shattered in spars and hull, the vessel goes
Near the safe port from every storm secured.

The road grows short; with frost or torrid skies,
By weary steps, hill, plain, and valley pressed,
Footsore and faint with toil the traveler eyes
The rising spire that marks the place of rest.

The night is near at hand; the shadow steals,
With the last sunbeam, farther from the trees;
In mist and chill the waning moon reveals
Her light, and hollow sounds the evening breeze.

The year is almost gone; the falling leaf,
Yellow and sere, flies far on every blast;
Spring flower, and summer fruit, and autumn sheaf
Gathered—its bright and beautiful are past.

Welcome! the port of refuge safe from storms,
Welcome! the silent city of repose,
Welcome! the night's dreams and visionary forms,
And winter's waste of purifying snows!

Another spring shall bloom; another day,
  Brighter than hope, shall rise to set no more;
A fairer region court the traveler's stay,
  And oceans, wreckless, spread without a shore.

Launched on their bosom, to each starry sphere,
  Beyond the reach of telescopic eye,
Farther than Fancy wings her swift career,
  Radiant, like suns, unbodied spirits fly.

Stripped of their fleshly rags—the mortal chain
  Of sensual appetite and passions vile—
Freed from the cankered earth, the sting, the stain
  Of base pursuits that dazzle and beguile,

Companionship with seraphim they hold,
  The endless chain of being they explore,
Nature's deep hidden mysteries unfold,
  And, face to face, the Ineffable adore.

Strong with the vigor of immortal youth.
  Beyond dim Reason's ken they speed their flight;
With Intuition's glance o'ermaster Truth,
  And find in knowing ever new delight.

Again, with earnest gaze and outstretched arms,
  They meet, oh thought of joy! the lost on earth,
Restored, renewed, arrayed in all the charms
  That Love bestows on Heaven's diviner birth;

Restored to part no more, no more to know
 The doubt, the fear, the change of mortal love;
To endless ages, hand in hand, they go,
 Sharing and doubling all their joys above.

Happiest of hearts on earth! the calm, the pure,
 Aloof from vulgar joys and vain pursuits,
That seek through life, unswerving, to secure
 Of nobler being these celestial fruits.

I ask no scholar's lore, no poet's lyre,
 Trophy nor wreath that conquerors display,
Nor wealth, nor wit, nor eloquence desire,
 Nor matchless wisdom, nor imperial sway,

But faith—strong faith—that upward to the sky,
 In every ill unshaken, undismayed,
Looks, like the eagle, with unblenching eye,
 Steadfast and bright in sunlight and in shade.

Let this be mine! and if the parting day
 Grow dark, the waves seem black with winter's gloom,
Fearless, though rough and perilous the way,
 I tread the path that leads me to the tomb.

LIFE

Along the lapse of years I look,
  From childhood on to feeble age,
And as in some old pictured book
  I read and turn page after page.
Few are the joys recorded there;
Its sorrows mark each passing year.

If childhood has its sunny hours,
  As poets say, I knew them not;
Or if they came, the fruits and flowers
  Withered and wasted are forgot.
The briers and thorns—the sneer, the taunt
And harsh rebuke—my memory haunt.

Youth's sanguine moments brightly gleam
  With hope—for me the hope how brief!
How soon the world dispelled the dream
  And turned the promised bliss to grief!
Cares like a murky mist to shame
And mar life's morning-glory came.

Its brilliant hours how illy spent;
  Its opportunities unused;
Buried or lost the talent lent,
  Neglected idly or abused;
Truth, knowledge, virtue's priceless prize
Forgotten in delusive lies!

The man's pursuits, the costlier toys,
  The scheme for fortune, power or place—
I tried them all—deceptive joys—
  Immortal natures they debase;
The fairest gaud the schemers know,
To spirit worlds how mean a show!

And household pleasures—how they fly!
  Death leaves his blighting footsteps there—
The fevered pulse, the glazing eye,
  The pallid face so cold and drear.
These, these, from memory never part,
But burn their traces on the heart.

Even as I write, mine eye and ear
  Recount the pang of pain, the groan,
The cry it wrings my breast to hear,
  The parting strife, the dying moan—
O that a father's love could give
A ransom that his son might live!

He's gone; but if to riper years
  The parent's pride and promise grow,
Do joys succeed to anxious cares,
  Does time the expected boon bestow?
Excess and vice the harvest blight
And shroud in clouds the morning light.

The coarse debauch, the reeking bowl,
The reeling step, the bloated face
Debase the mind, imbrute the soul,
And blast each youthful bloom and grace.
What are the wrecks of stormy seas
To wrecks of hopes and hearts like these?

What, though not all be blighted so,
What, in the flock, if ninety-nine
Escape or brave the noisome foe
And all their treasured love be mine,
Still, still, in ceaseless sorrow tost
I miss and mourn the one that's lost.

The mind's the body's waning powers,
The faith transformed to cold distrust,
The cheerless sun, the languid hours,
The buds of hope all turned to dust—
These fill the last dull dreary page,
The record of declining age.

Ah! who would tread his steps again
In life's deluding, changeful way
Of thorns and flowers, of joy and pain?
The thorns endure, the flowers decay.
Foreknown the coming weal and woe,
What light could hope herself bestow?

Thy better light, O God! reveal;
  Thy grace vouchsafe, Thy peace impart.
Thou givest alone the balm to heal
  The spirit bruised, the wounded heart.
Beyond the grave, above the skies,
I lift my weary thoughts and eyes.

Yet mine on earth one boon of Heaven
  To soften grief, to lighten care;
The choicest gift to mortals given,
  A loving heart to soothe and cheer,
Is mine—whate'er the ill may be
I closer cling, dear wife, to thee.

www.ingramcontent.com/pod-product-compliance
Lightning Source LLC
LaVergne TN
LVHW021410110826
845150LV00007B/1855